D0888939

Walk
with
the
King
Today

Dr. Robert A. Cook

Walk
with
the
King
Today

Dr. Robert A. Cook

CHRISTIAN HERALD BOOKS
Chappaqua, New York

Library of Congress Cataloging in Publication Data

Cook, Robert A., 1912–
  Walk with the King Today.

    1. Christian life—1960–   I. Title
BV4501.2.C673   248'.4   78-56977
ISBN 0-915684-42-X

First Edition
CHRISTIAN HERALD BOOKS, 40 Overlook Drive, Chappaqua, New York 10514

Manufactured in the United States of America.

To a family that has helped to make
walking with the King a reality...

Mildred, the sister who spent her girlhood days
caring for her motherless brother;

Coreen, God's perfect choice
for a very imperfect man;

Carolyn, Marilyn, and Lois, daughters
who have brought joy to our hearts;

Bestemor, my mother-in-love, whose life shed
the gentle glow of God's presence
throughout our home for many years; and
Charles and Daisy, Harold and Hilda,
parents who prayed.

Introduction

Part One
The Spiritual Walk

Part Two
The Personal Walk

Part Three
The Family Walk

Introduction

1. My Walk with Jesus the King

If—or rather since—"faith comes by hearing and hearing by the Word of God," my walk with Jesus the King must have begun a year or two before I ever trusted him as Saviour.

Some of my earliest memories are of the times when my sister Mildred would open the Bible and help me to pick out simple words that I could recognize. Words grew into phrases and phrases into sentences. By the time I was six I was reading my mother's huge Teacher's Edition of the Bible. She had slipped away to Glory when I was about 16 months old, and I owe to my father and my sister the fact that so early in life I began to get acquainted with the Bible and with the Saviour it presented.

Although my father was never quite the same after his Daisy died, he saw to it that his two motherless children had a home—and that he had the kind of job which would allow him to keep an eye on them. Working as a janitor in Cleveland Spencerian Commercial School, he received as part of his compensation a basement flat which became home sweet home to us in those days.

I did not realize then what it meant for a 15-year-old girl to keep house, bake bread, can fruits and vegetables, and go to high school, let alone keeping track of her "stroobly" haired, dirty-faced brother. I know now and have thanked God and my sister many times for the happy faith-filled hours I knew as a child.

I must have been about six years old when I trusted Christ as my Saviour. We attended the Christian and Missionary Alliance Church which met in a store building on Cedar Avenue. The church was presided over by a man who was later to become the Home Superintendent for his denomination, the Rev. H. E. Nelson. He was preaching one Sunday evening in his usual forceful and dynamic manner when I felt a deep longing to give myself to Christ.

I was seated with my father on the very last row of the store building auditorium, and the distance between myself and "the mourners' bench" seemed endless. When the pastor asked for decisions for Christ, however, I made my way to the place of prayer. There, with my father kneeling on one side of me and the pastor on the other, I trusted Christ as Saviour. Baptized shortly thereafter in Lake Erie, at old Beulah Park, I felt a deep awareness that something had been started which would make a difference all the rest of my life.

And it has!

One day shortly after my commitment to Christ, my father said to me, "Boy (he always called me 'Boy'—as Victor Borge says, 'I guess he couldn't remember my name'), how would you like to own your mother's Bible?"

My response was quick and sure. Yes, I would like to have that Bible, and yes, I would do anything I needed to do to get it.

"Tell you what," he said, "you learn fifty verses from the Gospel of John by the time you're seven and I'll give you that Bible, and a gold watch with it!"

I couldn't resist an offer like that, so I went to work learning a verse or two or three from each of the chapters in John's Gospel. And learn them I did. So you know there was one proud and happy boy when after reciting those fifty verses, I became the proud owner of that special Bible, plus a gold watch. The watch never ran very well, but it was gold, and it was mine, and that was enough.

All my friends know me as a "gadget man." I identify strongly with anything mechanical. Thus it is not surprising that during my junior and senior years in high school I began to tinker with automobiles. After a time I built up a small business overhauling the cars of friends and neighbors. This seemed to be the way I was to go after leaving high school. I would go to trade school, learn automobile mechanics and electronics, and have the biggest car dealership in Ohio!

Wisely enough, my father never disagreed with these plans and dreams. Rather, he suggested an alternate possibility which appealed to me at once. "You know, Boy," he said one day, "I don't particularly care what occupation you take up—banker, mechanic, electrician or whatever. But you'll be a lot better at whatever God leads you to do if you have some Bible training. Get some of that under your belt and then go on and be the best mechanic in the world! Tell you what I'll do," he continued, "I'll pay for a year at the Moody Bible Institute for you, if you want to try it. Then you can go ahead with further training in whatever field the Lord seems to indicate as his will for you. What do you say?"

As you can guess, it didn't take me long to agree to this proposition. So in August of 1928 I made my way to Chicago where the faculty of the Moody Bible Institute had made a special dispensation for this under-age boy to enroll as a student. My sister was living and working in Chicago so she could keep an eye on me. My father was going to pay for my room and board, which came to $9.65 a week (tuition was then, and still is, free at MBI), and I began to see great possibilities for both faith and fun in the future.

One does precious little philosophizing at age 16. I can see now, however, that God was leading me sovereignly in that step towards enrolling me at Moody. I did my share of "growing up" during those years and made my full quota of mistakes. I learned two great lessons, however. One was that to know and to proclaim what the Bible *says* is more important than hundreds of learned comments *about* the Bible. "Master what the Bible *says,* students!" said Dr. James M. Gray. "If you know what it says, you'll have little trouble with what it means."

The other great principle which has shaped my life is that

the supreme task of the believer is the evangelization of the world—beginning right where he is! Soul-winning was not left to chance at the Institute. We were assigned to what was then called "Practical Christian Work"—street meetings, mission meetings, jail services, hospital visitation, house-to-house visitation, youth meetings, and so on. Always, the emphasis was not on running the meeting, but rather on winning the lost to Christ, and then following them up with Christian nurture.

To know one's Bible, and to win the lost—that's what it means to be in Christian work. Yes, there are many other phases of ministry of which we are all aware; but I venture to say that these two principles form a pretty solid foundation for all the rest.

I never did forsake my love for cars. Even during the years at Moody I worked part time at a garage on Chicago Avenue. I would buy old junkers, fix them up and paint them, and then sell them at a profit. After graduation from Moody I worked full time at the car business, telling the registrar at Wheaton (Illinois) College that I would be enrolling in the middle of the school year—just as soon as I had made enough money.

I also had some musical ability which the Lord was able to put to his use. Two violin lessons a week for some years had provided me with a good musical foundation which I now used in directing church choirs.

It seems that a young pastor from Chicago's West Side was looking for a choir leader. He asked his friend, Evangelist McCormick Lintz, whether he knew anyone who could help out in that department. Mr. Lintz said, "There's a young fellow named Bob Cook who can lead a choir. You'll find him at 15 West Chicago Avenue in a garage behind an apartment house. He might be your man."

The result of this conversation was that while I was under a car working on its connecting rod bearings, a healthy kick reached my ribs, and a voice that sounded like a combination of grace and gravel spoke to me.

"Are you Bob Cook?"

"I am."

"Can you lead a church choir?"

"I can."

"Do you want to work for me?"

"I don't know—who are you?"

The speaker identified himself as Torrey Johnson, just graduated from Wheaton College, teaching Greek at Northern Baptist Seminary, and pastoring a small but growing Baptist church on Chicago's West Side.

My heart warmed to this young man. His bold and confident manner was undergirded by an evident love for God and for people. I could sense even then the dynamism which led him later to become the founder and first president of Youth for Christ International, and still later to be chosen as president and pastor of Boca Raton's fabulous Bibletown ministry.

The result of this exchange was that I became not only the choir leader, but also took on the chore of assistant pastor at Messiah Baptist Church. I lived in one of the Sunday school rooms, commuted daily from Chicago to Wheaton, and preached in a rescue mission twice a week just to keep my own soul warm.

Two things happened at this time which made a great impact on my life. Preaching in the rescue missions was one of them. Actually, I had done very little preaching throughout my years at Moody. Music was my field and whether I played the violin, led singing or directed choirs I felt content about it all.

One August night I was involved in a major car accident. A car traveling at high speed and without lights struck me with such force that my Model T Ford was overturned. As the trunk lid sprang open each of the neighborhood children helped themselves to a handful of my garage tools. By the time I crawled uninjured from the wreckage I was out of a car and also out of business.

I recall looking up into that summer sky and saying, "God, why do you do this to me?"

Fifteen years later I awakened to the fact that the start of my preaching ministry coincided with that traffic accident. God put me out of my business to get me into his business!

It was also during the days at Messiah Baptist that I fell in love. Pastor Torrey Johnson's wife Evelyn had a sister who sang in the choir. It didn't take me long to find a way to get introduced, then to see her home, then to consolidate, as we say, the friendship.

Contrary to all the success books, I doubt that many of us really plan our life and love in any detail. Rather, I think that daily yielding to God makes it possible for him to guide us in ways that he has planned for us. This was so in my case. While I was busy with cars, college, church and all the rest, God was leading Charley Cook's boy. First he led to high school, to Moody Bible Institute, then to the garage, the choir, the church, and finally to his choice of a life companion exactly suited for me.

Years later, Cedric Sears, who worked with me in Youth for Christ, summed it up. We were commenting on how wonderfully the Lord leads in one's life choices. Cedric said, "I certainly have to praise the Lord for the wife he gave me—and you know Bob, Coreen is an absolutely *perfect* Bob Cook's wife."

Amen, and Amen!

The years moved by quickly. Three daughters arrived to gladden our hearts and beautify our home. Each of them has grown up to be a testimony for the Lord and a joy to her parents. Carolyn and Marilyn were teenagers during the years when I served as president of Youth for Christ International. More than once, they were members of the winning Bible quiz teams, and, as part of their winner's award, accompanied me to the World Congress on Evangelization held in Venezuela. Lois came along several years later, and while not active in Youth for Christ because of our move to The King's College, she nevertheless followed up her childhood profession of faith with a life of sweet devotion and surrender to her Lord. As a nurse in a large hospital, she has a moment-by-moment opportunity to minister to hearts and bodies that are hurting with sickness, sin and sorrow.

I have spent 18 years as a full-time pastor, ministering in Glen Ellyn, Illinois; Philadelphia; La Salle, Illinois; and Chicago.

To be honest, I am sure I learned more from my dear people than they ever learned from me. God's people in the local church can sometimes be difficult, to be sure; but they are still the world's best people, and if one will love them and minister to them, they will reward him with a fellowship that is divine.

Walking with the King during those years in the pastorate taught me some valuable lessons. One was that you don't introduce new ideas suddenly and expect people to accept them. There has to be what the psychologist calls "ownership" of the idea. "You drop the idea as a seed thought after the adjournment of the meeting," my friend Vincent Brushwyler told me. "Then six weeks to six months later, some one else will bring it up as his own idea. Then you oppose it, and it will go through!"

Easy does it. I often tell young ministers, "Give yourself three years to introduce anything new. Meanwhile, just win one soul a week, and have that person ready to confess Christ publicly when you give the invitation on Sunday. Your church will grow ten percent a year, without any question."

Another lesson learned in the pastorate was that expository Bible preaching is the only way to "last" in the pastorate. Topical preaching becomes old with frightening rapidity; but the Word of God is ever new, and if one will specialize in giving out the Word, the Blessed Holy Spirit will see that it bears fruit.

Still another step toward maturity came when I learned that difficulties in the congregation will yield to prayer, when they refuse to budge under any amount of pressure or politicking.

I can recall being very upset about one of my church members who, let us face it, was in my opinion a catastrophe just waiting to happen. A well-meaning brother, he nevertheless gravitated unerringly to the most painful part of any discussion.

When urgings and suggestions failed, I finally took the matter to the Lord in a prolonged season of prayer. Strangely enough, I found that before I had been praying very long, I was confessing my own faults and needs under the gentle prodding of the Holy Spirit; and that I then followed such praying with intercession for this brother. Like Job, who was blessed "when he prayed for his friends," I too was blessed as I interceded for God's blessing upon my erring church member.

Did God answer? Yes, he did, and in ways that surprised and delighted me. In the process, the praying pastor got blessed! Years later, I can recall telling my young men in Youth for Christ: "Don't call a committee meeting—call a prayer meeting! Pray your way through the agenda, and you will have a shorter meeting. Use prayer as God's leverage for getting things done!" I learned that lesson from walking with the King in the pastorate.

In 1944 I was back in Chicago, working again with my brother-in-law, Dr. Torrey Johnson, as associate pastor of Midwest Bible Church. Growing out of a burden for the thousands of teen-agers who needed Christ, we started Chicagoland Youth for Christ. We met in Orchestra Hall, on Michigan Avenue, each Saturday evening. I led the singing, did the advertising, wrote much of the radio script, and made myself useful in general. This, of course, in addition to taking care of duties at Midwest Church.

A mass rally in Chicago Stadium and another in gigantic Soldier Field brought Youth for Christ to the attention of the

Christian public. In 1945 Youth for Christ International was formed with Torrey Johnson as president. He held this position for three years during which time I directed the Saturday meetings and pastored the growing Midwest Bible Church.

At the beginning of 1948, we saw a change in the situation. It was during that year that I traveled around the world with Merrill Dunlop and held rallies and campaigns in many nations. By this tour we hoped to stabilize the worldwide efforts of Youth for Christ.

That view of the mission fields of the world made an impression upon my heart and mind which has never faded. There are millions of people who have never heard the name of Jesus Christ and who do not know the God who "gave his only begotten Son" for them. To see and feel and know that men are lost is an awesome and unforgettable experience.

I came back from the mission field determined to do all I could to raise up men and women to go into the harvest fields of the world for Christ. I found that God was leading me out of the pastorate and into the ministry of Youth for Christ. This troubled me and I began to seek the Lord for an answer to this problem. How was I, a pastor, going to do anything other than pastoral work if I was going to be true to my calling?

The answer came one night as I knelt by my bed in a tourist home in Ohio. I was on a series of one-night meetings. I was bone-weary and was about to have a very brief devotion before dropping into bed. I told the Lord that I was still waiting for an answer to the meaning of the changes I could see taking place in my ministry. Directly the answer came. I had been reading the fourth chapter of John. Now the words seemed to leap out at me from the page. "I sent you to reap that whereon ye bestowed no labor: other men labored and ye are entered into their labors." At that moment God was clearly saying, "Your job in these coming years is to reap the harvest that is ready all across the world."

My entire view of Youth for Christ was changed that night. I saw as I had not seen before that the work of the local church and the work of the missionary can be helped and complemented by harvesters. These laborers must see to it that converts are channeled back into the Christ-centered, Bible-believing church of their choice.

There was another major change in my life in 1948. At the annual Youth for Christ Convention in Winona Lake, Indiana, I was elected president of the organization. The change from pastoring and leading Chicago's YFC rallies was challenging and a bit scary. Managing YFC was, as one man put it, "corralling a bunch of race horses." In the nine years that followed, however, I found again and again that God will never ask me to do something for which he also does not enable me. Those years saw the start of high school Bible clubs, now called Campus Life clubs. It was also the beginning of what we call "One-country-at-a-time evangelism"—an all-out concerted effort to reach an entire country with the Gospel. Latin American Mission was to call it "Evangelism in Depth" and would successfully reach many areas with this method.

Youth for Christ started as a sporadic religious phenomenon. It was now growing up. New young leaders were being brought up through the ranks and were learning, gaining experience and succeeding.

God is the perfect teacher, and he taught this student many valuable lessons during those years at Youth for Christ. Some of these lessons were easy to learn. Some of them were very hard. They have all been rewarding.

God uses a man, not a machine. In the beginning of YFC, and all through the following years, God chose men like Torrey Johnson, Billy Graham and the many others who labored with them. God gave the man a vision and what followed was the outworking of that vision by the enablement of the Holy Spirit.

Prayer is the price of leadership. Prayer is also the atmosphere through which a God-given directive can be applied. Many of the crucial decisions made in the councils of Youth for Christ came out of all-night prayer meetings. I cannot remember one single prayer-bathed decision that we ever regretted.

Evangelism is the catalyst that breaks down barriers of selfishness and prejudice. Christians, even those with widely diverse backgrounds, can work together if they will pray and if they will concentrate on evangelism. In the world congresses on evangelism we found that after an entire night spent in prayer our hearts were tender and people were prepared to work together to win the lost.

Personal devotions are the stuff of which effective public ministry is made. Faced with a schedule which often included as many as 8 or 10 meetings a day (I once had 13!) I found that the only way to survive spiritually was to meet with my Lord in the early morning. The busier the day the earlier I needed to arise. Skip that morning meeting with the Lord and the rest of the day would net me very little. But get something fresh from the Lord in the morning and I could share it throughout the day with great effectiveness.

Neglect of personal, private meetings with the Lord led me inevitably to failure. One of the saddest things in the world is to see the decline of a highly gifted ministry—a ministry that is falling to pieces for want of a daily meeting with the Lord. A person in this plight starts to work harder, fails more often, becomes more critical of others, and finally turns to cynicism and bitterness. This kind of decline is both tragic and needless.

Change isn't wrong if God is in it. I learned that lesson from a dear friend, Mel Larson, now with the Lord. Mel was serving as editor of the Youth for Christ Magazine, and I often shared my concerns with him. On one occasion I was complaining that many of the YFC leaders had branched out into their own ministries—leaving me feeling somewhat alone.

"Change isn't wrong if God is in it," he told me. "And look at what God is doing through Billy Graham, Cliff Barrows, Bev Shea and the others. Look at Greater Europe Mission founded by Bob Evans. Look at World Vision founded by Bob Pierce. God had something great for them, and he hasn't forgotten you."

Gradually I began to realize that I was becoming more weary after each extended trip to Youth for Christ ministries across the country and around the world. I began to seek God about the next step.

Incidently, I had written a number of goals for my life some years before. One of these mentioned some contact with religious publishing. Another cited the possibility of a school where one could multiply his usefulness in the lives of young people.

So it was that in 1957 I started work as vice president of Scripture Press, in Wheaton, Illinois. Five years there taught me how to budget, how to manage by objective, how to be aware of costs and what Dr. Cory, founder of Scripture Press, used to call "the missionary margin." Repeatedly, I was reminded of the immense power of the printed page— power to change lives and to move people heavenward.

In 1961 I was contacted by William Miller, chairman of the board of Trustees of The King's College in New York. Mr. Miller, now with the Lord, had heard from Bev Shea that "Billy Graham thought Bob Cook might make a good president for King's." Some months went by, and a visit to Briarcliff Manor, New York, produced an invitation to become the president of The King's College.

Now I was faced with two questions: Did I want to accept the challenge of leading a college which needed regional accreditation, financial stability and continuing spiritual renewal? And also did I want to risk failing, in case it didn't work?

This had been the hardest decision of my life so far. To accept meant pulling up well-established roots in the Midwest and assuming a leadership position for which I had not been formally trained. (I was to learn later that for the most part college presidents are not trained, but rather discovered.)

I think my greatest fear was that if things did not go well all my friends around the world would be saying, "Too bad Cook couldn't make it go . . . never should have tried it."

Finally one day as I prayed in my study in Wheaton, I was led to say to the Lord, "I guess I don't have to be a success. I guess all I have to do is be faithful. Lord, if you want me at King's you can have me."

Then peace came, and a decision was made which has never been regretted.

All of this illustrates my firm belief in Proverbs 3:5-6. If you really want God's will, and seek it, *that's what you'll get.*

Part One
The Spiritual Walk

2. Dare to Pinpoint Your Prayers

Now that I've told you something about my own walk with Jesus Christ, I want to share some of the spiritual foundations on which my walk with the King has been based. One of the basic principles has been personal conversation with my Lord.

Some say that if you're a good enough Christian you'll never have any trouble. Everything will always be all right. Even though you're going through trials, you'll always be chin up and smiling.

Well, I've found that life is a little different from that. I've found that some of the best saints get discouraged and get upset. Paul, certainly no slouch at Christian living, said, "We would not have you ignorant of our trouble which came to us in Asia, that we were pressed out of measure, above strength, insomuch that we despaired even of life."

You and I have said the same thing. We do go through troubles, and we get upset by them. We get tied in a bowknot with anxiety. We get to the point where we want to scream, "I can't stand it anymore."

That's when we need to pray, James says, "Is any among you afflicted? let him pray" (James 5:13a). Pray when you're in trouble.

I'm amazed at the vast number of people whom I've met who don't pray until they bump up against something that really hurts them. Then they suddenly detour around that hurt. Prayer, if it doesn't get to the point, is just a speech we make to God.

Maybe you can't get along with your mother-in-law. She's absolutely impossible, you say. Have you ever dared to pray, "Oh, God, I can't stand that dear woman. I'm married to her son, but I can't stand her. She picks on me and she's getting on my nerves. I just can't take her. Now Lord, do something about it!"

Have you really prayed honestly to God about your
trouble? I think it would do us a lot of good to tell God
accurately and honestly what is disturbing us. James says to
pray. And that means to pray earnestly; pray pointedly; pray
in detail.

A missionary friend told me about being evacuated during World War II from an island where he worked. He was
put on a freighter which zigzagged through the desolate
areas of the Pacific. They saw no other ships until one day
they spotted the periscope of a submarine peeping at them.

"That's when I learned to pray specifically and in detail,"
my friend tells me. "While he was looking at us and probably
wondering whether or not to sink us, we were praying over
every inch of that submarine. 'Lord,' we prayed, 'stop his
motors, jam his torpedo tubes, break his rudder!'"

This man prayed pointedly and in detail. His life was at
stake!

Do you want to take the sting and the steam out of
trouble? Take it to God and pray it through. Don't just say,
"Lord, help me." But pray through the situation. Analyze it;
take it apart. Bring it to God piece-by-piece.

Verbalize to God the fact that you're hurting, you're in
trouble, you're scared, you're in danger or your world has
fallen in upon you. This will take the steam out of the
pressure cooker. Your circumstances may not change, but
you will be different. God will give you no detours out of
your trouble. But he'll do something inside you to make you
a different person in the trouble.

Pointed prayer is God's method of getting things done.
"In everything by prayer and supplication with thanksgiving let your requests be made known unto God" (Philippians 4:6). That's the divine order. Prayer is worship; supplication is pleading; thanksgiving is praising the Lord. And this
combination adds up to victorious praying.

We need to pinpoint our needs before God. Too many

times we forget that he is interested in the details of our life. Most of our praying is quite banal because it is so general. We pray safe prayers, phrasing them so that if nothing happens we won't lose face. Listen to some of the prayers you hear in prayer meetings and you'll be amazed at the generality and the shallowness, the banality, pointlessness and repetitiousness of much of our praying.

Now I know God listens to all our prayers. The lisping of a little child is as important to him as the ponderous prayer of the theologian. But effective praying means pointed praying.

Do you dare verbalize to God the things in your life that ought to be changed? Do you dare tell him the needs you feel? I find it difficult sometimes to verbalize these things. And when I have this difficulty, I write out what is bothering me. Then I look at what I've written and ask myself, "Is this exactly the case? Does this really say it?"

When I'm satisfied that what I've written expresses what I honestly feel, I bring it to God and say, "Now, God, this is it." Sometimes I read it to him. Other times I lay aside my paper with its careful phrasing and play it back to God in my own words. But I pray pointedly. And it makes a difference!

Pointed praying means you give some thought to your request. We can all improve our praying if we'll list those things that are really important. Do you have a prayer list? Make a specific list and keep praying day-by-day until God answers and you can write a big "Hallelujah" alongside the request. This kind of pointed praying lets the faithful Spirit of God zero in on your need.

Have you analyzed your situation and brought it to God piece-by-piece? Have you prayed it through? Good! Then keep on praying. Don't quit! Keep on praying a few minutes after your mind has said, "I've got to get out of here."

Your mind often stops just short of God's blessing. Every person has his own built-in attention span. Learn to push yourself beyond this point. Especially when you're praying about something that's breaking your heart, keep on praying honestly and earnestly a few minutes beyond the point when you normally would quit. Instead of giving up and saying, "Well, I've prayed," keep on praying for just a few minutes. Pray persistently and see what God will do for you.

Then praise God. That's right, praise him even in your trouble. Can you dare to try that? You're probably backing off a little and thinking, "Brother, you don't know what kind of trouble I have. Who could praise God for that?" You can argue that point if you wish. But I'm simply saying that praise works. "In everything by prayer and supplication *with thanksgiving* let your requests be made known to God."

When you're in trouble, look up and praise God. "In everything give thanks." If you stop with supplication—pointed praying—you're cutting short God's plan for blessing.

Many of us, I think, close the door to the Almighty's working in our lives because we neglect or refuse to praise God when we pray. Praise opens the door of faith. Praise lets me abandon myself to God just as I am, in the situation where I am and with the shortcomings I know I have. I see the depressing reality. But when I turn and praise God for it, I open the door of faith. Praise lets my spirit fly out of the cage of unbelief. Through praise I can soar out into the great, open skies of God's wonder working.

The next time you pray, start praising God. Maybe you're ill, but you can still get around. Praise God! Maybe you have problems with your kids. But you do have them and the enrichment they've added to your life. Praise God! Maybe you have problems with your job, but you still have a job. Praise God for it!

Then by faith praise him for handling your case now. Praise in the present tense assures future victory. Have you prayed to God in trouble? Have you pointed out specifically where you want him to work? Then praise him. You know by faith he is working for you. This is victorious praying. Then when you've learned how to pray, you're ready for some additional steps, some new dimensions in your walk with the King.

3. New Dimensions in Your Life —by Faith

When I was young, my father used to say to me, "My boy, I have to provide food, shelter, education and loving care for you. That's part of my job. But," he went on, "that isn't all. We have to build a life—*your* life—you and I. And there's something *you* have to work at, too, my boy!"

We all know there are some things you get "for free," and others you have to work for.

Every one of us who is God's child begins with certain clearly defined dimensions in his walk with the King. This is precisely the point that the Apostle Peter makes in 2 Peter 1:1-8. He says God has given to us his grace, all things "that pertain unto life and godliness," along with "great and precious promises" which are the key to Christian character and a holy life.

Notice that Peter goes on to say, "And beside this, *add* to your faith . . ." Add what? Virtue . . . knowledge . . . temperance . . . patience . . . godliness . . . brotherly kindness . . . love. Peter is saying, "Give some thought to the extension of the boundaries of your Christian life." But remember that these new dimensions come not by your trying, but by your applying *faith* to the particular areas of your life.

What Do We Begin With?

We receive some things from God by faith, without our working for them.

. . . His grace is free: "By grace are ye saved, through faith, and that not of yourselves, it is the gift of God, not of works lest any man should boast," God gives us saving grace, keeping grace, enabling grace, sufficient grace, grace to live and grace to die.

. . . God's peace is free, too—"peace that passes all under-standing." You can't define it, weigh it, or nail it down, because it is altogether divine. But you can experience the wonderful supporting strength of it! Peace is the quality of *God*, entering into your very nature.

. . . God's joy is free. Jesus said, "These things have I spoken unto you that my joy might remain in you, and that your joy might be full." "Full" means running over. Your cup may be small, but it can overflow a lot! "My cup," said the psalmist, "runneth over."

. . . God's power is free. In answer to the question, "What kind of power?" we go to the Apostle Paul who says that the power that works in the believer is the same power that "God wrought in Christ, when he raised him from the dead." Resurrection power is ours—even now.

. . . God's equipment for the Christian life is free. "According as his divine power hath given unto us all things that pertain unto life and godliness, through the knowledge of him," Peter says.

There isn't anything that you will ever need to enable you to live the Christian life that has not already been given to you. It's yours!

Are you aware of how rich you really are?

You remember the story of the couple who were taking their first ocean voyage. They had scrimped and saved to get enough for their steamship tickets. Then, they thought, "We must plan for food for the journey." Carefully they measured out cheese and bread and some dried meats—all they could afford—enough, they hoped, to last until their destination was reached. Day after day they doled out the daily ration and ate it solemnly in their cabin.

Just before the trip ended, someone discovered that these people had been eating alone in their cabin and inquired why they did this. When this old couple explained that they were trying to make the food last until the voyage was completed they were told, "Why, all your meals were included in your steamship tickets! You could have been eating as much as you wished, every day."

You get the point. All you need for a blessed, fruitful, satisfying Christian life is already yours. Claim it! Make it your own!

Stimulant for Awareness

How does one appropriate the "all things" of which Peter spoke? We do it through getting better acquainted with the Lord, and through the application of his Word to our life.

"All things that pertain unto life and godliness" become real to us, first, "through the knowledge of him." This means personal, intimate knowledge, as one has of a close friend. Spend time with your Lord, and your character will be modified heavenward.

Second, appropriate the promises in God's Word. Let your soul feast on the thought that God forgives your sin, he makes you his child, he opens up heaven to you, he gives you over 30,000 promises in the Bible as your very own, and then, as if that weren't enough, he takes his very nature and gives *that* to you, and then undertakes to live his life through you!

I know from personal experience that God's Word in the mind and heart make a difference in one's attitudes and decisions. While I was a pastor, on one occasion, shortly after I had embarked on a vigorous program of Bible memorization and meditation, one of my deacons remarked, "Hey, preacher, your preaching is different—what happened to you?" "Whatever it is," he went on, "keep it up—I like it."

You can try this practice for yourself—and you'll find it works. Take some 3 x 5 index cards. Cut them in half and write a Scripture verse with its reference on each of these handy 2½ x 3 cards. Then place the cards in a location where you will look at them several times a day. . . over the sink . . . on a mirror. . . in your wallet. When you glance at the Scripture verse, say it aloud, with the reference. In between times, think about what the verse said. By so doing you will be giving God's Word a chance to penetrate beyond your

conscious mind and memory, into the "computer" portion
of your mind from which the Holy Spirit can recall it when
needed.

So there you are—all these things given to you . . . free.
But don't just stand there, looking. Appreciate! Appropriate! By faith—you and God working together—extend the
borders of your Christian life. Peter goes on to tell how this is
to be done. He says, "Besides this (that is, all that you
already have from God) . . . giving all diligence, *add* to your
faith . . ." Diligence is a great word, not used much in our
day.

What Does It Mean To Be Diligent?

Briefly stated, to be diligent means "Get on the job . . .
work hard at it . . . stay with it until the task is done."

Diligence means thoroughness. Thorough, that is, as in
housecleaning. Few married men can ever understand why
the ladies have to dig into corners, tear everything up and
pull everything down, but diligence demands it.

Diligence also means completeness. Don't quit until the
job is done. Many a person, in the pressure of some trial, or
under the conviction of some great spiritual experience, has
started a life of dedication to the Lord's will. But somewhere
along the line, he or she has quit. It is time for us to renew
our consecration, to consider *finishing* the job.

Small thought here: Learn the value of spending an extra
few minutes in prayer. When your mind says, "Time to say
'Amen,' Let's get out of here to the work of the day," quietly
wait before the Lord a little longer. In those *extra* moments,
you give God a chance to break through in your life and to do
a precious work of his grace. This is diligence in prayer—
keeping at it.

Some Things You Can Add to Your Life by Faith

Faith as an additive is a valid scriptural principle. The
Apostle Paul says (Colossians 2:6): "As ye have therefore received Christ Jesus the Lord, so walk ye in him."

How did your Christian experience begin? It began by faith, of course—simple, uncomplicated faith. How do you proceed to grow in your relationship with God? Again, by faith. And it is faith applied in all the varied situations that you face every day. You don't live a whole day at a time, do you? Life breaks up into little segments, like pieces broken off a loaf of bread. For each of those pieces of life, so to speak, you and I must form the habit of trusting the Lord Jesus Christ with the same abandonment of ourselves to him that we had when we came to him for salvation.

Peter lists some of the items to be "added."

1. . . . Add to your faith—knowledge.

There is some knowledge for which you have to dig. I tell our students at The King's College that a prayer meeting is no substitute for doing your homework. God will never, in answer to prayer, help you to remember something you did not first learn. Nor will he, in answer to prayer, bypass his Word and reveal directly to you the truths that you could find by reading your Bible.

There is another kind of knowledge that comes by faith, as God blesses his Word, and the Holy Spirit applies it to your life. That knowledge is an intimate acquaintanceship with the Lord Jesus Christ. "Acquaint now thyself with him, and be at peace," we read in the book of Job.

Here is a mysterious and yet a wonderfully thrilling truth. When next you go to your knees to speak with your Lord, say to him, "Lord Jesus, just as I trusted you as my Saviour, so now I want to trust you to reveal yourself to me while I read your Word and wait before you." I can promise you that such prayers are never unanswered.

Years ago, while I was a guest in a lovely home, I was also the victim of an agonizingly busy schedule. I soon found that if I were to survive the pressures, I had to meet the Lord early in the morning, before the family awoke, and get something fresh from the Lord to feed my own soul—something which

I could share in the three to seven meetings I had each day.

Early one morning, while I was seeking the Lord, I was nearly panic-stricken to find that the time was going by, my hosts would soon be awaking, the day would begin, and I still had nothing fresh from God's Word.

I remember praying earnestly, "O Lord, hurry up! There's not much time left!"

Precisely at that moment of my urgency, the Lord graciously opened up the Scripture passage I had been studying and gave me a whole heartful of truths which I shared joyously throughout the rest of the day.

See the glorious combination: Truth—propositional knowledge—is yours if you will dig for it in the Word. Triumph—dynamic, personal knowledge—is yours by faith, if you will pray and believe for it.

2. ... Add to your faith—virtue.

Virtue is the quality of being spontaneously good. This is goodness that goes beyond the hope of reward. How do you achieve it? Simple: When the Lord Jesus Christ becomes Lord of your life, then his desires become your desires. The psalmist exclaims, "I delight to do thy will, O my God. Yea, thy law is within my heart." There is a dynamic principle at work within the believer's life. Paul states it in Philippians 2:13: "For it is God which worketh in you both to will and to do of his good pleasure." To will—that supplies the want-to. To do—that supplies the power. God does both for you when *his will* is your highest priority.

Once when my daughters were very young, we went as a family to enjoy a special celebration meal at a restaurant; I think it was a birthday. We looked over the menu. Almost at once I knew what I wanted, and so did Mother and our older daughter. But the younger one, about three and a half or four years old at the time, was uncertain. To tease her, I took the big menu and put it under her face and said, "O.K., dearie, what would you like?"

Her eyes filled with tears and she looked up at me and said, "Papa, I just want what you want!"

Well, at that point she could have had the whole world with a pink ribbon around it! You know that. What God is waiting for from you and me is just the glad declaration, "I want what you want." That is "virtue." We obtain it by faith.

3. . . . And to your faith—temperance.

"Temperance" means, literally, inner strength. This is the strength of God working in our lives through faith. Paul prayed for his friends at Ephesus that they might be "strengthened with might by his spirit in the inner man." Let's get away from the idea that temperance is some kind of restrictive self-control that we impose upon ourselves. Scriptural temperance is not self-control but rather God-control. It involves our bringing to him the areas of our life that need changing.

Here is a practical suggestion:

Make a list of the things in your life that you have never been able to handle—the ones that always defeat you. Bring this list to God in prayer. Verbalize honestly to him about those areas where you have been victimized. Then start *trusting* him to change each defeat into victory. I can promise you that he will.

God may not always change your circumstances in answer to prayer, but he will change *you*—in the circumstances—and make you a victor instead of a victim.

Consider the other areas of life listed for us in 2 Peter 1:5-7. At first glance, I agree that they present an almost impossible challenge.

Patience: The art of staying under, and not blowing up or giving up.

Godliness: The quality of God in the everyday experiences of life.

Brotherly kindness: The ability to go beyond the concept of "fellow man" and to look upon others as our true brothers and sisters . . . to treat them as members of the family of God, with us.

Love: Calvary love, "shed abroad in our hearts by the Holy Spirit." This is the "love" of John 3:16.

A formidable list, is it not? The answer to our achieving victory in all these realms is found in our getting at the task, and submitting, by faith, every part of our life to the almightiness of God.

It took the greatest of all miracles to save you, did it not? Can you not trust God for the additional miracle of building your life into that which is Christlike and God-glorifying?

Add to your faith! Then, as my deacon said to me, so your friends will be saying to you, "Hey, you're different! What happened to you? It's *good!*"

These are some of the spiritual flagstones on which the Christian walks with the King. Now I want you to look more closely at your own walk with Christ and think about some of the ways you can be a blessing.

Part Two:
The Personal Walk

4. For Such a Time as This

Your own spiritual life reaches its most beautiful blossoming when you honestly and genuinely believe that God has deliberately selected this part of the 20th century as the age in which he wanted you to serve him and his people.

God has always raised up certain individuals for a particular place in history. Joseph was raised up for his day, David for his. Daniel was God's nominee for prime minister, by way of the prisoners' barracks. To Queen Esther came the call of God through her cousin Mordecai: "Who knoweth whether thou art come to the kingdom for such a time as this?" (Esther 4:14). With the clear light of centuries shining on the story, we are sure that Queen Esther was God's provision for the needs and crises of her people.

One person—and God uses that one to affect the many. There was just one Abraham, just one Elijah, just one Peter, just one Paul, just one Augustine, just one Luther, just one Moody, just one Hudson Taylor. And there is just one you!

Have you ever thought what your life might mean to those whom you can influence—either for good or for evil? One Ahab—and a nation sunk in idolatry. One Josiah—and a nation led in revival! Who knoweth whether thou art come to the kingdom for such a time as this?

But, you say, who am I? Moses said the same: "Lord, I am not eloquent." Gideon was far from convinced by the angelic commission: "Wherewith shall I save Israel? I am the least in my father's house." John the Baptist, busy about his God-given ministry, had no time to spare to reflect on his greatness; yet of him the Lord declared, "Among them that are born of women there hath not risen a greater. . ." (Matthew 11:11).

God is looking for those who will allow him to work

through them. "I sought for a man among them," he says, "that should make up the hedge, and stand in the gap before me for the land, that I should not destroy it: but I found none" (Ezekiel 22:30). "Run ye to and fro through the streets of Jerusalem, and see now . . . if ye can find a man, if there be any that executeth judgment, that seeketh the truth; and I will pardon it [the whole city]" (Jeremiah 5:1).

Who can forget Moses' prayer, burning with the eloquence of a desperate heart? "Oh, this people have sinned a great sin, and have made them gods of gold. Yet now, if thou wilt forgive their sin—and if not, blot me, I pray thee, out of thy book . . ." (Exodus 31, 32:32). God looks for someone who will stand between him and a city—or even a whole nation. And that someone could be you.

Responsibility is implicit in the Christian message. The believer is responsible for himself and his relation to God's truth: "Take heed to thyself and to the doctrine . . . so then every one of us shall give account of himself to God." The believer also is responsible for his brother: "Judge this rather, that no man put a stumbling block or an occasion to fall in his brother's way." And the believer is responsible for his world: "God is not willing that any should perish, but that all should come to repentance. . . . Go ye therefore."

The Christian is to make a difference in his world, as long as he is in it. Our Lord said to his disciples, "Ye are the light of the world . . . ye are the salt of the earth." He also said, "As long as I am in the world, I am the light of the world . . . as my Father hath sent me, even so send I you."

Above all, we who are privileged to enjoy a great deal of light and liberty certainly are more responsible under God than those who are less favored. It is about time that fat, sleek, easy-going American believers take stock of their situation, and faced their duty to the rest of the world! "For unto whomsoever much is given, of him shall be much required" (Luke 12:48).

For such a time as this . . .? What kind of time do we live in? Basically, the world, the flesh and the devil are no different from what they were in other centuries. Sinful human nature is still predictably selfish, anti-God and anti-good. Human personality in the raw is still "filled with malice and envy, hateful, and hating one another." We need not expect the world to love us Christians when it hates our Christ. We need not expect the great men of our day to come flocking to the Cross; "not many wise men after the flesh, not many mighty, not many noble" respond to his call.

A Confused Time

Some characteristics, however, seem to belong especially to the day in which we live. One is that it is a confused time. No one seems sure of anything. Having thrown out authoritative religion, together with faith and belief in the inspiration of the Word of God, modern educators and scientists have fallen prey to the philosophy of tentativeness—thinking that what is true today may not be true tomorrow, since some new satellite may loom up over our horizon and change all our concepts.

Even in religious circles many are hiding their confusion under the guise of "having an open mind." The person with religious convictions is accused of being a bigot. The New Testament believer who knows what—and Whom—he believes is labeled as naïve, obstructionist and reactionary.

Yet it is the open-minded who succumb most quickly under the pressure of mind and spirit. Hunter says it was the men who were college- and university-trained in having "an open mind" who collapsed the soonest under the pressures of Communist brainwashing. They weren't sure of anything—so they had nothing to live or die for. Luke says that in the end time "there shall be . . . upon the earth distress of nations, with perplexity" (21:25).

Christians do well to identify this characteristic of the age in which we live and decide where they stand in relation to it. Because others are confused and are surrendering, one by one, the principles for which our fathers stood and which they affirmed with their own blood, does it follow logically that we too must be just as confused and that we must give in to the drift of a godless world? Never!

It is the enemy that whispers, "Surrender . . . give up." It is the Spirit of God speaking through the believer who says, "None of these things move me, neither count I my life dear unto myself, so that I might finish my course with joy, and the ministry, which I have received of the Lord Jesus, to testify the gospel of the grace of God" (Acts 20:24).

So others are confused? Let them be. You stand for something! You are somebody—a child of the King! You know him through the miracle of the New Birth! You talk to God every day, and he talks to you! Your steps are divinely guided, and your life is divinely protected, so that nothing evil can harm you! Your standards of life are already set by a Holy God, and forever settled in his Word—good enough to live and die by!

Let the world wobble on its foundations; you stand firm on the solid Rock, Jesus Christ. Let others wonder what to believe—you make sure that you know what and whom you believe . . . and that you believe it strongly enough to stake your very life on it!

History has never been written by discussions. People who like to hear the sound of their own voices rarely can be counted upon to lead a faltering humanity out of its troubles. It is the Bible-based stalwart who dares to say, "Sirs, I believe God!" that makes all the difference in the midnight of a shipwrecked world. Thou art come for such a time as this!

A Corrupt Time

The second thing to consider is that we live in a corrupt time. There are, for example, the phonies. Matthew 24:24 speaks of those who will "deceive the very elect." Peter warns of some whose speciality is "beguiling unstable souls," who "through feigned words make merchandise of you." Paul warns that in the last days there will be those who have a form of godliness but who deny the power thereof. They are all with us today.

There are the fallen-away. Luke 18:8 asks the plaintive question, "When the Son of man cometh, shall he find faith on the earth?" And Matthew 24:12 flatly says that the love of many shall wax cold. One would have to admit that about the only thing most evangelicals know of sacrifice is how to spell it. A drifting coldness, like the imperceptible chilling of the blood before death by freezing, is sweeping over the visible church. Much religion . . . little heart.

There are the forsaken. Iniquity shall abound, Matthew says. Paul paints the horrible picture of people so wedded to their sin that they call black white and call wrong right. Dialectic materialism is simply the logic of the damned—put in a book! God is forced to forsake such people. "God gave them up," says Romans 1:24, 26, 28.

Every so often the F.B.I. warns that crime is increasing. But we have lived with a rising crime rate for so long that we count it like rising prices—inevitable—and go on living with it. Standards are sagging, morals vanishing, and godlessness is taught to our society in little doses through mass communication media. We are living to see the day when God is turning his back on people who have forsaken him. "The wicked shall be turned into hell, and all the nations that forget God."

Yes, it is a corrupt day we live in. But what about you, child of God? Thou art come to the kingdom for just such a time as this!

Others are false. Do you have to be? No! Paul says, "Be henceforth no more children, tossed to and fro, and carried about with every wind of doctrine . . . but speaking the truth in love, . . . grow up into him in all things, which is the head, even Christ. . . . Walk not as other Gentiles walk, in the vanity of their mind . . . , having . . . given themselves over unto lasciviousness, to work all uncleanness with greediness" (Ephesians 4:14, 15, 17-19). Someone has to be true, no matter how many counterfeits there are! You be that someone!

Others have fallen away. Should you? No! "Hold that fast which thou hast, that no man take thy crown" (Revelation 3:11). The secret of avoiding apostasy is not fighting apostasy, but fighting sin and Satan with the sword of the Spirit—the

Word of God! If more apostasy hunters would take unto them the whole armor of God and go out after lost souls, rebuking sin and Satan, we would soon have a different climate in the church of the Living God! "Take unto you the whole armor of God, that ye may be able to withstand in the evil day, and having done all, to stand" (Ephesians 6:13).

Others have given in to the ever-encroaching spread of godlessness. Must you? No! "When the enemy shall come in like a flood the Spirit of the Lord shall raise up a standard against him" (Isaiah 59:19). Who knoweth whether thou art come . . . for such a time as this? It takes just one person, sold out to God, filled with his Spirit, to make all the difference.

A Challenging Time

We live also in a challenging time. These are terrifying days—catastrophe is just a heartbeat away. Some madman can at any moment loose upon the world a holocaust that would, within the space of thirty minutes, leave fifty million Americans dead. People are losing their minds through sheer panic . . . "for fear, and for looking after those things which are coming on the earth." Many a heart attack is being induced by constant fear, that brings the tension that stops the beating of life in the breast.

And yet, for the child of God who is walking in the will of God, there is—or ought to be—perfect peace and an opportunity for service such as he has never known before. Are people afraid? He has the antidote to fear: One, a Person, who says, "I will never leave thee nor forsake thee" (Hebrews is today! You have the priceless privilege of presenting him to people who are confused, corrupted, caved-in emotionafter that have no more than they can do . . ." (Luke :4).

The death of the body is just an incident in the eternal story of divine accomplishment. To die is to depart and be with Christ which is far better. The great longing is not to live long, but to live—or to die—in a manner that will glorify Christ.

If ever the Lord Jesus Christ was real, he is today! You

have the priceless privilege of presenting him to people who are confused, corrupted, caved-in emotionally and spiritually spent. You are come to the kingdom for such a time as this. God has plans for you. God have mercy on you if you back away from living—or dying—so as to make a difference in the history of your generation!

Let us be fully cognizant of the force of prophetic truth, and the cast of coming events foretold in God's Word. But let us never forget that in the economy of God, the seemingly inevitable march of human events has often been reversed by one person who dared to believe and obey God! Remember Moses . . . and Elijah . . . and Daniel . . . and Peter . . . and Paul . . . and Luther . . . and Wesley . . . and Edwards . . . and Finney . . . and Moody! Remember Joseph . . . and Gideon . . . and David . . . and Hezekiah . . . and Nehemiah! God is still saying, "Ask me concerning my sons, and concerning the works of my hands, command ye me . . . ask what I shall do for thee . . . according to your faith be it unto you . . . ye have not because ye ask not."

Oh, Little-faith, the issue is not whether you live long or comfortably, whether you are spared war and its suffering or whether your taxes go up or down. Eternal matters are at stake! You are responsible for projecting God into the day in which you live. Your Sunday School teaching and preaching must communicate God! Your life must be a demonstration of what God can do in shoe leather! Your personality must always be plugged into the heavenly switchboard!

And through it all, God is willing to tie his almightiness to your faith. Make your plans and your prayers big enough for God to get into! Specialize in believing and obeying God in your own life—leave the projection of it across the world to him.

Who knoweth whether thou art come to the kingdom for such a time as this? Make your life count for Christ the King by walking in the power of his resurrection.

5. Resurrection Power—Do I Have Any?

Once a year, at Easter, the whole Christian world gives at least nodding assent to the fact that Christ is alive.

But the resurrection of Jesus Christ is much more than a repetitive remembrance. It is the crux of the Good News:

> . . . the gospel . . . that Christ died for our sins according to the scriptures; and that he was buried, and that he rose again according to the scriptures . . . (1 Corinthians 15:1, 3, 4)

Actually, every Sunday is Easter. More than that, every day that we Christians live we are to have and to show the mighty power of the risen Lord.

But is this true of us?

The very possibility humbles us. We feel like praying:

> Thank you, Lord, for Easter . . . Thank you for Jesus . . . Thank you for the resurrection . . . And thank you most of all that the blessed Spirit of God makes Christ real in our lives day by day . . . Oh, may this be our individual and personal experience . . . May the living Christ be so excitingly real to us that we cannot help but share him with others. Amen.

To be honest, evangelicals—you and I—never sound so phony as when we are talking about the resurrection. This is not because we do not believe that the resurrection of Jesus Christ is an historical fact. We do believe it. And it's not because we've forsaken this blessed doctrine which is the cornerstone of our faith. We hold it very dear. You could get into a red-hot argument with almost anybody on our college campus if you suggested that we forsake the doctrine of the

46

bodily resurrection of Jesus Christ. But we sound phony oftentimes because we have very little personal experience of the resurrection in our lives.

Criteria for Determining Genuineness

There are many criteria for knowing the real from the phony. Currently in vogue is love for one's brother. We sing:

> They will know
> We are Christians
> By our love.

Those words have reference of course to John 13:34, 35 where the Lord Jesus said, "A new commandment I give unto you, That ye love one another . . . By this shall all men know that ye are my disciples, if ye have love one to another."

However, love is not the only criterion for determining what is real. There are many others in the Word and if you take them all together, it's quite an order!

The Lord Jesus said, for example, "Herein is my Father glorified, that ye bear much fruit; so shall ye be my disciples" (John 15:8). In other words, fruit-bearing is one important proof of true discipleship. It could very well be said that if you are not winning somebody to the Lord Jesus Christ on a regular basis—not just talking about it but doing it—there may be some doubt as to the reality of your relationship to him. Something to think about!

Furthermore, the daily walk is intensely definitive—separating the real from the counterfeit. John remarks (1 John 2:6): "He that sayeth that he abideth in him ought himself also so to walk, even as he walked." This says to me that my lifestyle needs to be discernibly Christ-like if I say I'm a Christian.

Paul the Apostle had a great yearning to "know" Christ: "That I may know him, and the power of his resurrection, and the fellowship of his sufferings . . ." (Philippians 3:10). For Paul, the proof of really knowing Christ was the personal possession of resurrection power, Calvary compassion and a Christ-like daily walk.

The first of these, resurrection power, has been upon my mind for the past many hours as a subject for our consideration together.

We are faced with the question: Resurrection power—do I have any of it? The lack was not limited to the Ephesian believers. Sadly, it has existed as long as the church has been on earth. Paul prayed that the

> eyes of your understanding (be) enlightened
> . . . that ye may know . . . what is the exceed-
> ing greatness of his power . . . which he
> wrought in Christ when he raised him from
> the dead . . . (Ephesians 1:18-20).

To put this truth another way, Paul was saying: I want you to have a personal experience of the resurrection.

Greek students will at once identify that word "know" as coming from the Greek word *ginosko* which means to know something deeply, personally—experientially, if you will—not merely academically or intellectually.

Now I have to tell you in all frankness—though you already know it—that this kind of knowledge of Christ is a rare and scarce commodity among 20th-century believers. Yet that condition could be quite different if we wished it so. Ephesians 2:1 goes on to say, blessedly:

> And you hath he quickened who were
> dead in trespasses and sins; wherein in the
> time past ye walked according to the course
> of this world, according to the prince of the
> power of the air, the spirit that now worketh
> in the children of disobedience: Among
> whom also we all had our conversation in
> times past in the lusts of our flesh, fulfilling
> the desires of the flesh and of the mind; and
> were by nature the children of wrath, even as
> others . . . (Ephesians 2:1-3).

New Life for the Total Person

Where are the areas of deadness where resurrection power needs to operate? The first is one's way of life: "... wherein in time past ye walked...." The word "walk" means, quite simply, to live day-by-day. One's whole manner of living needs divine resuscitation. I can't tell you what that will mean for you, because I don't live inside your skin. You know, however, what your real lifestyle is and in what ways and to what extent it needs resurrection power.

In a Christian school such as The King's College, it is quite possible for one to learn to comply with the rules and regulations sufficiently to get by. Mere compliance stands you in no advantage whatever in the business of daily living. What God wants—and what I think most of us who have a heart for people also long for—is not mere compliance with the letter of the law but a day-by-day demonstration of the mighty power of God in the life. As an individual, you alone can figure out where resurrection power is needed.

Isn't it strange how we hanker for the world, generally? Paul said that Ephesian Christians "walked according to the course of this world." Their lifestyle was geared to the world, as ours often is. And yet when Jesus Christ takes control of a life, all of the attractions of the world system begin to fade, and the things I've been fighting for and arguing about and griping over and complaining of—all of them appear in new perspective and become minuscule in size and importance compared to other things that Christ brings into focus.

This re-assessment of values has come to me personally many times, and I'm sure it has been the experience of some of you, too. What matters is not my relationship to the dead standards of the world culture around us, but to the standards of the living Christ within us. Here is where resurrection power must begin to show. I ask myself: Is this true of me? Is it true of you?

New Life for My Daily Walk

What else needs resurrection? I need a different spirit to control my life. I need to remember that the Ephesians "walked according to the course of this world." The word "according" comes from a little Greek word *kata* which means "right down along the line." In other words, they were living right down along the line of the course of this world—a world culture dominated by "the prince of the power of the air, the spirit that now worketh in the children of disobedience." It is a frightening thought that you can be a Christian and at the same time allow your life to be largely controlled by the spirit of the age. What can remedy this distressing condition? Not legislation, certainly, but resurrection. I need divine life infused into my heart and mind, into my emotions and my will, so that my daily life will reflect his power within me.

New Life for My Mind

What else needs resurrection? Paul says the Ephesian Christians were "fulfilling the desires of the flesh and of the mind." This is true of us also, all too frequently. The "I want" and "I will" and "I won't" that emerge from my mind need resurrection, that is, control by the Spirit of God.

There is nothing wrong with my having a mind and exercising it. There is nothing wrong with having a little steel in one's backbone. But rigidness in itself profits little. The strong mental attributes that we possess need to come in contact with the living Christ and be brought into glad submission to him.

There is nothing so sad, it seems to me, as to see a person who claims to be a Christian but whose mind is still a slave to his own desires. It is twice deplorable, I say, because it is so needless and because it is a travesty on the whole concept of Christian living.

The Lord Jesus Christ didn't come down the stairways of stars to Bethlehem and walk to Calvary and break his heart for the world's sin—your and mine in particular—in order that we might somehow limp in through the side door into Glory, having been a slave to our own wants and to the spirit of our age throughout our lifetime. No, the plan of salvation is far greater than that. It is his plan to "always cause us to triumph in Christ" (2 Corinthians 2:14). That statement presupposes that resurrection power is at work in your mind. Let me ask you: What is driving you? Is it your thoughts, your own desires, or is it the Spirit of God who is motivating you day by day?

What Resurrection Means

Paul tells us in Ephesians 3 what resurrection means.

1. Inner Power

First of all, resurrection means the possession of inner power. Paul said he was praying for the Ephesian Christians,

> that he would grant you, according to the riches of his glory, to be strengthened with might by his Spirit in the inner man ...
> (Ephesians 3:16).

There is no question in my mind that when one is born again, the Holy Spirit comes to dwell in that life. "If any man have not the Spirit of Christ he is none of his" (Romans 8:9). We are born of the Spirit, sealed by the Spirit, baptized by the Spirit (John 3:5, 6; Ephesians 1:13, 14; 1 Corinthians 12:13). We are also to be infilled by the Spirit (Ephesians 5:18)—allowing him to touch and fill and move through every area of our life.

It is a pity, however, that we keep him, as it were, in the front hall, never allowing him to occupy all the nooks and crannies of our heart-house.

Let us suppose that you are a visiting minister, as I have been many times. You arrive at the home where you are to stay for a few days of the meetings in which you have a part. You are a little early, perhaps, and the lady of the house greets you with panic in her face and curlers in her hair. You sense it: Things aren't quite set for the visiting prophet.

Your hostess says, "Oh, do come in and make yourself at home."

What she really means is: Stay over there in the corner and don't make any noise.

So you sit down. You are very quiet. You don't make any waves. Finally everything is ready. The family gathers. You have dinner, you go off to the meeting, and let us say that you are encouraged by the good response there.

You come back to your host's house. They put on the coffee pot and you have "a little fellowship."

"Now we'll show you to your room," they say. You see at once that it's Junior's room. He's sleeping on two chairs, mad as a wet hen. But this is your room for now.

The meetings go real well. By and by you are on a first name basis with the people who are entertaining you.

But one day comes that is different from the others. The man of the house says to you, "Could I show you my carpenter shop in the basement?" Sure, you're glad to see it. And it's great!

Then he says, "I'm using all these tools to build a new bedroom for the boys in what used to be the attic. Wouldn't you like to see it?" Yes, you'd like very much to see that.

So you go up the stairs, and you look at the construction area and the plans your host explains to you. All of a sudden something strikes him.

"You know"—he looks at you as though he had never seen you before. "Could I call you Bob? You're just like one of the family."

You're in! It took a week to get there. But now the hearts and the house are all wide open.

The Holy Spirit is waiting too. He's waiting for some of us to have the good sense to say, "Spirit of God, come in. Come into all the rooms of my heart-house. Come into the room where my failures are. Come into the room that houses the habits that drive me. Come into the room where my hopes and ambitions are lodged. Come into the room of nameless things that I try to keep from you and from people. Oh, Spirit of God, come in!"

Welcome him into your life. Get to know the power—not just the fact, not just the doctrine, not just the dogma, not just some poor dead profession that has behind it the stinking corpse of your personal failure—get to know the power of the resurrection in your life.

What will happen then? Christ will be at home in your heart. He will be established there. You have to admit—don't you?—that the Lord Jesus might not be quite at home in some of the areas of your life. Are there some "rooms" where you would be embarrassed to invite him in? Well, the answer to that is, Let him in! He will make the necessary changes. You never need to be afraid that he will cheat you or harm you or give you less than the best.

We have seen then, that resurrection means the possession of inner power.

2. Awareness of Christ's Love

Second, resurrection means personal experience of the love of Christ. We are to

> comprehend with all saints what is the
> breadth, and length, and depth, and height;
> and to know the love of Christ, which pass-
> eth knowledge . . . (Ephesians 3:18, 19).

A personal experience of the love of Christ comes when you let God fill all the rooms of your heart-house. Strangely, your awareness of the love of Jesus Christ is directly proportional to your willingness to let him fill your life. It is a sobering thought that every area from which you exclude him becomes the means for constricting you in your awareness of his love. Oh, you can talk about him without full commitment to him, but the words will have a thin, brassy sound. They won't really mean anything to people around you because there's nothing there to back up what you say.

But when you allow Jesus Christ to operate in your whole

person you'll have a corresponding increase in the divine
electricity of God's love flowing in and through your soul—
"overflowing" is the word. "Filled," Paul said, "with the
fullness of God." The word "filled" means filled to capacity,
running over. You find the idea in Psalm 23: "My cup runneth over." Most of us, if we minister at all, draw from the
dregs at the bottom of the cup. We have nothing better to
give. We have never given our all, first, to Christ.

Why not minister to other people out of a blessed overflow? What people want is the bubbling, quenching grace of
God for their thirsty souls. Witnessing is not so much a skill
to be learned as a spillover to be shared—your personal
delight with the Lord Jesus Christ. Nobody wants to be
proselytized. Nobody wants to be converted from one religious position to another. But everybody is hungry for the
love of the Lord Jesus Christ and your sharing of him, if your
own experience is real.

Are you dipping into the empty, leaking cistern of reli-
giosity, or are you offering the sweet waters of the over-flow-
ing cup? Jesus came, he said, to put within us artesian wells
of blessing: "He that believeth on me, as the scripture saith,
out of his innermost being shall flow rivers of living water"
(John 7:38).

That's what resurrection is all about. It is not merely
affirming that something phenomenal happened 2,000 years
ago. Of course it happened! Thank God it happened. Thank
God for the empty tomb and the angel announcing, "He is
not here; he is risen." Thank God for that. But oh, shouldn't
it show up in my life? Of course it should, and by God's grace
it can, at every step.

3. Ceiling Unlimited

Third, resurrection means unlimited power in the individual life.

We might say, resurrection means "ceiling unlimited."
Paul ascribes praise to God with these opening lines: "Now
unto Him that is able to do exceeding abundantly above all

that we ask or think according to (here it is again) the power that worketh in us. . . .''

What kind of power is this? Resurrection power! How much of it? No limit!

How much have you asked God for? I can guarantee it isn't enough. Most of us don't have a complete enough or a deep enough or a truthful enough prayer list—praying not only for people and organizations but also for deep inner needs of ourselves and of others. We pray about things that it is convenient to pray about. We pray in vague terms, largely because we think that, if nothing happens in answer to our petitions, we won't lose face. To know the power of the resurrection is to realize that there is no limit to what God can do in and through us.

All of us learn early in life that we have certain limitations. Our I.Q. limits us. Our background, our training, our reaction to changes—all these things limit us. But when you're dealing with God there isn't any boundary to what he can do through you.

Recently I re-read the story of George Mueller, that great man of faith, raising thousands of dollars for the upkeep of his orphan homes. One morning there wasn't anything to put on the table for his hundreds of dependent children and no money to buy anything—and he never went into debt. He just said, "I'm going to trust God and lead the children in giving thanks to God for the breakfast that isn't here."

There came a knock on the door and a man said, "The bakery wagon broke down and I can't deliver these loaves. I wonder if you can use some fresh bread."

Someone else came to the door and said, "We have some fresh milk here. I wonder if you can use it."

Did these things just "happen"? No. They were answers to Mueller's ceiling-unlimited prayer of faith. God can take an ordinary man or woman—and most of us are pretty ordinary, aren't we—and do extraordinary things through us, in the power of the resurrection.

Make this a time of transformation in your life. Make it a

time when you're done with the old dead things that belie
the very faith you profess to have. Make it a time when Jesus
Christ becomes real in your life. He's able to do exceeding
abundantly above all that you ask or think. Ceiling unlimited! He'll never say, "You've asked too much this time." No.
Go ahead. Ask him. Yield to him. Open the door of your
heart-house to the Spirit of God and get to know for yourself
the power of resurrection in your life. That's what makes the
difference between orthodoxy and genuine spirituality.

6. Orthodox Or Spiritual?
There Is a Big Difference

Probably one of the biggest hang-ups for the present generation is the disappointment and frustration people experience when they discover that orthodoxy and spirituality are not always the same.

We have always tended to mistake the form for the fact, the resemblance for the reality. And this problem will show up at the Day of Judgment. "Many will say to me in that day," our Lord warned, "'Lord, Lord, have we not prophesied in thy name? And in thy name have cast out demons? And in thy name done many wonderful works?' And then will I profess unto them, 'I never knew you: depart from me, ye that work iniquity.'"

In other words, there always have been and always will be people who mistakenly think that doing or saying certain things (or not doing or saying them) mark them as acceptable with God.

Our Lord Jesus had some highly explicit things to say about those who, in his day, were "orthodox" in the sense of outward performance only:

- These people are chiefly interested in seeing others keep the rules (Matthew 23:4).
- They are intensely interested in their public image. Good works, for them, are "to be seen" (v. 5).
- Their unbelief keeps them from reality with God and causes others to stumble (v. 13).
- They think that increasing the output of piety ("long prayers") will cover up for ruthlessness and greed (v. 14).
- These folks are busy, but there is no blessing in their ministry (v. 15).
- Spiritual standards are something to be wrapped

57

around prevailing values—for instance, gold or the gift of the altar (vv. 16-19).

• Their orthodoxy involves great devotion to trifles and neglect most of "the weightier matters of the Law—judgment, mercy, and faith" (v. 23).

• Probably the most telling criticism of all was our Lord's remark that these folk, for all their orthodoxy, were guilty of outward shining and inward sinning! They indulged in fatuous and exaggerated sentiment over the wrongs of the past, while continuing in their own evil ways (vv. 25-31).

All of which is to say that orthodoxy, by itself, can be dead; and that dead orthodoxy is often characterized by special attention to trivia, eagerness to enforce "the rules," permissiveness, rationalization of unconfessed and unforsaken sin, and a chronic busyness which misses the mark of eternal truths and values.

When It's Real

1. A person who is spiritually "real" will be excited about what the Lord Jesus Christ has done for him.

Before you dismiss this statement as a truism, check off in your mind the number of people who can honestly say that Christ has changed them. Not too many, are there? Paul describes the difference for which we are looking: In times past, he says, you conformed to the culture in which you lived, you were enslaved by the appetites of your body and your mind, and you naturally did things which merited the judgment of a holy God. Now, God has made you alive, and you are different (Ephesians 2:11-13).

Now, he says, instead of lying, you tell the truth. Instead of unchecked temper, you are under God's daily control, and sundown finds you reconciled with your brother. Instead of stealing, you labor productively. Instead of dirty talk there is conversation that builds up spiritually. Instead of unforgiveness and bitterness, there are forgiveness, tenderness and love. Instead of immoral practices, there is a positive morality, which specializes in goodness, righteousness and truth (4:17-29).

Most people use small daily situations as the basis for measuring another person's spirituality. A missionary friend tells of an unsaved interpreter who was converted to faith in Christ after he witnessed the missionary's total lack of resentment after the interpreter had appropriated their one blanket on an exceedingly cold night!

Blankets . . . resentment . . . what kind of standard is this? It is the ruthless, factual standard set by the people around us. They want to see whether our so-called faith really works—whether it makes any difference.

Unsaved people know they are deficient in the moral, the religious and the social areas of life. Paul sums up these deficiencies by listing what he calls the work of the flesh:

Moral: Adultery, fornication, uncleanness, lasciviousness.

Religious: Idolatry, witchcraft, seditions, heresies.

Social and interpersonal: Hatred, variance, emulations, wrath, strife, envyings, murders, drunkenness, revelings, etc.

A child of God had better show a discernible difference in these measurement areas if he expects people to believe him.

2. A person who is spiritually real will not grieve the Holy Spirit and will bear the fruit of the Spirit.

Much of the brassy, hollow sound of our Christian testimony can be traced to the fact that we have grieved the Holy Spirit by some sin we have permitted ourselves. We feel we cannot give up our indulgence, whatever it is. So we keep on going through the motions of "religion"—without the Spirit's power.

Bitterness, wrath, anger, clamor, evil speaking, malice, unkindness, hardheartedness, unforgiveness, lack of love, and immorality grieve the Spirit.

Spiritual reality—and spiritual power—depend on facing these areas honestly and submitting them to the work of the Spirit. When the Holy Spirit fills your life, someone has said, he will make you holy and spiritual.

Incidently, when the Holy Spirit is in control, the Lord Jesus Christ will be central in the focus of every life situation.

Non-Christians "seek their own," and Christians seek "the things which are Jesus Christ's." The big difference is not how much but from whom!

3. A person who is spiritually real has no hesitation in trusting any situation entirely to God.

Say what you will about Simon Peter, he was willing to risk obeying the command of Christ. Whether it was casting a net awkwardly into the sea after a fruitless night of fishing, or putting a size 14 foot over the side of the boat when Christ said "come," Peter was willing—and the Saviour saw him through!

Where do we begin in making relevant this matter of risking something on the Word of God? Probably the best place would be where we show the most unbelief—in our everyday lives.

Do you know anyone who prays before he answers the phone? Or before he opens a letter? Or writes the reply, for that matter? What child of God do you know who prays about his action on a personnel form at the office, or about the preparation of a routine report, or the formulation of a sales presentation? Who thinks of "obeying God's will" when beginning a casual conversation or an official conference?

Pray about *That*?

Face it: We reserve our contact with the will of God for areas that are unimportant, and which for the most part have no connection with our daily lives. This is why unbelievers around us do not fall in line to find out about our Christianity. They notice that it doesn't have much effect on us!

The areas of greatest concern to those in their teens and twenties are acceptance by their peers and dating someone who will impress their friends. Suggesting that one pray about these matters may be greeted with the same enthusiasm as suggesting that we all get vaccinated for smallpox.

For people who are in the age bracket generally termed "adult," the areas of concern involve money, status and security. Talk to some of your friends about this matter, and see how many of them react with total shock to the idea that a person should risk anything as important as money or job security on the will of God! After all, let's not run this thing into the ground!

One remembers the surprise and criticism voiced some years ago when a brother left his high-salaried job as editor because he would not work on a publication that advertised liquor. "What a pity!" someone said. "Why couldn't he have stayed there and been a testimony?"

Leaving a job is risky. It is daring, regardless of the potential cost, to obey God. Not many Christians are willing to undergo such risk.

New Testament Christianity has a holy contagion all its own. That element is faith in motion. Faith has always been willing to face the "What if . . .?" factor. Shadrach, Meshach and Abednego had started as captives, but they were now "over the affairs of the province of Babylon"—a high responsibility indeed. Upon their answer to King Nebuchadnezzar's question had depended not only this career, but their very lives. Would they risk it, or would they take the second chance the king had offered?

"We are not careful [care-filled, worried] to answer thee in this matter," they said. "If it be so, our God whom we serve is able to deliver us from the burning fiery furnace, and he will deliver us out of thine hand, O king. But if not, be it known·unto thee, O king, that we will not serve thy gods, nor worship the golden image which thou hast set up."

In the last analysis, your willingness to risk the "What if . . .?" factor is the test you must pass if you would impress people who are going where the action is! That willingness determines whether you are a yes man or a man of conviction.

7. Do Your Convictions Show Or Are You a Yes Man?

> "The greatest part of mankind have no other reason for their opinions than that they are in fashion." —Samuel Johnson

> "And be not conformed to this world; but be ye transformed by the renewing of your mind, that ye may prove what is that good, and acceptable, and perfect will of God."
> —Romans 12:2

Conformity, the new standard of 20th-century excellence, is as old as the very human desire to be accepted by other human beings.

Conformity (giving in) under social, or management, or domestic pressures has now become the norm of value and the standard of acceptance with others.

What a pity! One has the feeling that if Christ died only to make me more expert in bowing to the wishes of others, Calvary was in vain.

And yet, there it is—we may as well face the fact that success in our day seems to depend upon the skill with which we adjust to the desires and prejudices of others. The personnel director of a multi-million dollar corporation, when asked what quality he looked for first among executives, answered, "Adaptability—they must become part of the team, or we can't use them."

To put it boldly, a man gives in first to the force he is most afraid of. Anxiety, according to the business experts, is responsible for a high percentage of increased performance among employees. And anxiety, let us admit it, is nothing more than fear with an aspirin in its mouth!

If you want to follow that logic further, the fact that we

are so anxious to please people may well be proof that we are not as anxious to please God as we ought to be.

How does it come about that young people who don't like the taste of liquor nevertheless take their first drink? Or that a boy who knows smoking his first cigarette will make him throw up, still smokes it? Or that a girl who knows her purity is the only thing that makes her a worthy choice for wifehood, nevertheless gives away her honor—doesn't sell it, just gives it away under the pressures of another's desires?

Because most of us are more afraid of other people than we are of God; and we want to please people more than we want to please God.

Joseph had a secret. He said, "How then can I do this great wickedness, and sin against God? . . . I fear God!" (Genesis 39:9, 42:18)

Just what makes a conviction, anyway?

Information

"This is the way it works," might well be the starting point for a good set of Christian convictions.

"If ye love me," our Lord said, "keep my commandments. He that loveth me not keepeth not my sayings." This is the way it works: Anybody who loves Jesus obeys him.

"Whosoever is born of God doth not commit (practice) sin." This is the way it works: Anybody who is saved doesn't keep on in it.

"We know that we have passed from death unto life, because we love the brethren. He that loveth not his brother abideth in death." This is the way it works: Anybody who is saved has God's love for other Christians in his heart; and if he doesn't, he isn't saved.

"Know ye not that the friendship of the world is enmity with God? Whosoever therefore will be a friend of the world is an enemy of God." This is the way it works: Anybody who really loves God is not going to be friends with the world's crowd.

Information keeps us in line, when we decide that it is

absolutely basic. You don't poke your finger into electrical outlets, because you know how electricity works. You don't linger in front of a moving train, because you know how the law of force works. You don't jump off a high building because you know how the law of gravity works. You eat nourishing food because you know how the law of nourishment works.

If we lack convictions, it could be that we have never taken the trouble to find out the basic information about God that is available in the Bible.

Exclusion

This is the *only* way it works. "But without faith, it is impossible to please him; for he that cometh to God must believe that he is, and that he is a rewarder of them that diligently seek him." This is the *only* way it works.

"God is a spirit, and they that worship him must worship him in spirit and in truth." This is the *only* way it works.

Bob Pierce told the story of Korean refugees who discovered that by scraping the soft growing layer of wood cells off the trees, they could boil up a sort of soup that would fill their starving bellies. So they would come up to the lumber mill, wait until the stripping machine had taken the outer bark off the trees, and then would scrape into their cooking utensils this soft layer of wood cells. They would feed this preparation to their children and to themselves and then die of starvation.

Why?

Because the human stomach is not built to digest cellulose. It will handle human food, but that is the *only* way it works.

Spiritual life and issues are much the same. You may have all sorts of acceptable compromises and substitutes, but unless you have real convictions based on "This is the *only* way it works," you are in for trouble.

A Healthy Fear

"If I try any other way, I shall get into trouble."

Back to our original point: We give in to the things we are most afraid of. The fact that our generation has lost its fear of God, its wholesome reverential awe of God, is largely responsible for our pitiful effort to please people. "The fear of man bringeth a snare," said the wise man, "But whoso putteth his trust in the Lord shall be safe."

A Sense of Responsibility

"Other lives are involved in everything I do!" "For none of us liveth to himself, and no man dieth to himself... judge this rather, that no man put a stumbling block or an occasion to fall in his brother's way." "It is good neither to eat flesh, nor to drink wine, nor anything whereby thy brother stumbleth, or is offended, or is made weak." "Whoso shall offend," said our Lord, "Whoso shall offend one of these little ones which believe in me, it were better for him that a millstone were hanged about his neck, and that he were drowned in the depth of the sea."

Yes, others are involved, and my Lord holds me responsible! All the gilt-edged excuses in the world cannot explain away a life that has been smudged by my own carelessness or compromise. Real convictions will always think of the other person as well as one's self.

If you've read this far, you are probably wondering, "Well, what do I do about it? You can't just grab convictions out of thin air!"

Right you are! But you can start where the psalmist did (Psalm 119:59): "I thought on my ways, and turned my feet unto thy testimonies."

He thought about himself, and where he was headed. So should you!

He took steps in the direction of God's will—so must you, not alone for the sake of having convictions that will stand the test of social and business pressure, but for a life that stands the test of eternity, as well! Depression is often the result of a life that lacks convictions of this kind.

8. Life Is Just Too Much for Me....

Everyone knows and likes good old wishy-washy Charlie Brown. But follow this little fellow of comic strip and now TV fame, and you'll find him down in the dumps about half the time—especially after his team has lost another ball game, 110-0!

Even Charlie's more lively friends get depressed from time to time. Linus goes into the depth of despair when he loses his blanket. Lucy is always getting fed up with Charlie. Snoopy becomes irritable when he's disturbed from his restful perch atop his doghouse roof.

You know what it's like, too, to be down. Maybe your folks just don't seem to understand you. You're discouraged with your looks, or your weight. Nobody ever asks you out. You car breaks down before a big date. You pulled a bad grade. You flubbed up in the big game. You're uncertain about the future. Or you're just feeling generally low, maybe for no apparent reason.

What Causes Discouragement?

What causes these low ebbs? Why can't life be one great big up, without the downs? And how does a person climb out of the doldrums?

For some insight on the causes of discouragement, the Bible is an important source.

There is a phony, pseudo-discouragement, for instance, growing out of overriding personal desire and lack of spiritual discernment. The biblical example is Esau, and the situation is as follows:

Esau has been out hunting and comes home famished. He smells the tantalizing odor of stew cooking over the fire. Jacob, on being asked to give Esau a big helping, says, in effect, ''Not so fast! There's a price on this stew—it's your birthright.''

Now comes Esau's classic comment: ''Behold I am at the point to die: and what profit shall this birthright do to me?'' (Gen 25:32). And he sold his birthright to Jacob.

Actually, Esau wasn't dying; he was just hungry. Combined with this hunger was a tragic lack of appreciation for the spiritual blessing contained in the birthright. The Bible says, ''Esau despised his birthright.''

Be careful lest, when you say, ''I'm discouraged—I give up,'' that it is not a reflection of your desire to give up in order to have your own way!

Closely aligned with Esau's attitude is that shown by Jonah. After he had reluctantly made his way to Nineveh, preached sermons on impending judgment and seen a city-wide revival, he sat down and asked God to take away his life. This is discouragement born of not getting one's own way. When this happens to you, back off from the situation and ask God to show you things as they really are—as he looks at them. If Jonah had seen Nineveh as God saw it, with countless precious souls at stake, he would have had little time to complain!

Elijah was another who became discouraged. His attack of this spiritual virus came—as it does to many of us—at a time when he had just passed through a great victory and when he was physically exhausted. To add to the situation, he had just received the word of the wicked queen that she had vowed to kill him. So, ''when he saw that, he arose and went for his life, and came to Beer-sheba . . . left his servant there. But he himself went a day's journey into the wilderness, and came and sat down under a juniper tree: and he requested for himself that he might die'' (I Kings 19:3,4).

God, faithful and tender as always to his servant, saw to it that Elijah was fed and rested and then revealed himself to his servant in the ''still small voice.'' Elijah came back from that experience of discouragement stronger than ever.

Jacob was discouraged because circumstances seemed to be against him . . . Jeremiah was discouraged because no one would listen to his preaching . . . Job was discouraged because of personal sorrow and suffering.

What To Do About It

What should you do about discouragement?

Get acquainted with your moods. Many a situation you think is absolutely impossible may not be so desperate as it appears. You may simply be having one of your low days; you may just be down in the trough. You'll find, if you keep track of your feelings for a while, that your moods follow a cyclical pattern, alternating between feeling "high" and "low" in cycles of a few days to two weeks or longer. Someone has said, "Make your plans when you're high and evaluate them when you're low, but always know which is which."

Find your own discouragement spots and learn to live with them, and if possible to avoid them. If you drive a car along a certain road each day and if you know there is a deep hole in the road at a certain place, you may hit it once, but after a few jolts, you'll learn to steer around it. Life is like that. Just learn to steer a little.

Discouragement will yield to facts, a plan of action, prayer and the steps of obedience! Wait on God, get his perspective and plan, start obeying by taking the first step of action and discouragement will vanish!

Remember that discouragement is contagious! You can catch it from others, and they, in turn, can be infected by your own attitude.

You don't have to stay miserable unless you'd rather be that way. Some people are spiritual hypochondriacs. They would rather be down and sad than take the steps that would effect a cure and make them happy. If you are that kind of person—well, you'll just have to stay blue.

Blues are often a result of being preoccupied with one's self. Focus on others, their needs, burdens, hopes and fears, and your blues will vanish!

Remember that many times your physical condition gives rise to your emotional reaction. You may feel blue and realize later that it was not your troubles or the world around you that was at fault, but just that you were catching a cold or were extra tired.

Reading a favorite portion of Scripture and praying will do wonders for your moods. Praise is especially effective. When you feel as though you have reached a new low in life, take a few moments to praise your Lord and see how the mists of discouragement clear away!

You can also be of help to a friend who is discouraged. Just don't try to give advice. Instead, listen. Ask questions. Let your friend know that you know how he feels—not by saying so, but by just sharing his feelings inside your own heart. Get your friend started on a train of thought and action that is positive and constructive. If it helped you to get your thoughts off yourself and on to another's woes, why not another person.

Try to guard your friend from taking impulsive actions "on the rebound" of discouragement. Most of our mistakes are made in a hurry! Take time to wait. Wait on God, wait on yourself, wait for time itself to make a difference. Never make a decision when you are ill, angry or discouraged. You are almost certain to regret it later.

Above all, if you want to offer lasting help to your friend, get him in touch with God through the Word and through prayer. Trust God with him and for him, because prayer changes things. Listen to David: "I found trouble and sorrow. Then called I upon the name of the Lord; O Lord, I beseech thee, deliver my soul. I was brought low, and he helped me. The Lord hath dealt bountifully with thee. For thou hast delivered my soul from death, mine eyes from tears, and my feet from falling" (Psalm 116:3-8).

After all, the cure for discouragement is found in a Person—your blessed Lord. Knowing him, talking things over with him and taking the steps of obedience to him as he leads—this is the secret. Why not take inventory right now, and reset those dislocated priorities?

9. What Does 'All for Jesus' Mean?

One of the things we need to do in the matter of steward-ship is re-examine our own value system. A person will inevitably follow the values he thinks most important.

In the third chapter of Revelation our Lord Jesus remarks to the Laodicean church, "Thou sayest I am rich, and increased with goods, and have need of nothing; and knowest not that thou art wretched, and miserable, and poor, and blind, and naked."

Everyone who is responsible for some aspect of God's work inevitably has gnawing at the edges of his mind the consciousness of his responsibility. We think in terms of fixed costs and payrolls and budgets and people and equipment and programs. At the same time we might well ask ourselves in a tough-minded fashion, "What really is valuable to me?"

On one occasion I spent a whole week inventorying my work as a pastor. I made a list of everything I was doing and alongside of this, its comparative value in terms of eternity. I found that a great deal of my regular schedule as a fairly methodical person did not have any discernible value in those terms.

Take an Inventory

It would be excellent for every one of us to inventory our values. What really blesses us? What upsets us? What do we worry about? If we lie awake sleepless, what keeps us awake? What do we laugh about and what do we gossip about and what are we really driving for? What are our values?

We are probably the best equipped bunch of professing

Christians that ever came down the path of history. We have all the gadgets and equipment and more money per capita than most of the people who went before us in spite of the fact we are reaching for still more. What are the real values? Examine your own values. Stewardship has to follow values.

Many a minister needs to do this in terms of his relationship to his organization, his church and his family. What is really valuable—being at x-number of committee meetings or speaking at x-number of luncheons or raising x-thousands of dollars, or maybe spending a little time with your 10-year-old? What is really valuable—being known with the district superintendent as a highly promising young man who ought to be recommended for the next vacancy at the "First Church of I will Arise," or seeing that the Holy Spirit of God by his power delivers somebody who is a slave to sin?

Reset Priorities

We ought also to reset our priorities. If you want to find out what is important, ask who should drop dead last and you will easily know. There are some things that can wait. There are other things that ought not to wait. The priorities of the Christian life have a definite bearing on how much support we are going to get from God's people.

I have worked with a board nearly all my life. I have been turned down by church boards and other kinds of boards at different times. On one occasion I laid out a whole first edition of a church newspaper and brought it to the deacons' meeting and submitted it to the brethren. They looked at me and said, "Young man, we brought you here to preach the gospel, not to publish," and they promptly killed it. I had a brief period of mourning, stayed mad for a little while and then forgot it.

However, I have never been turned down by a board anytime, anywhere, for any reason when I had established something as a God-given priority born out of earnest prayer and I knew the Lord had told me to do something.

Once we have settled priorities under God the thing has to go. This matter of stewardship follows a kind of holy desperation that says, "God told me to do this and I have to do it!"

This is the authority of the ancient prophet Amos. We can see him in our mind's eye. His fingernails had never known a manicure. His hair was long and straggly. He had a voice like a foghorn, homespun garments and the long, mile-eating stride of the outdoorsman.

He went across the miles, reached the king's court and said to the first guard, "I have a message for the king." "Pass on in." Second guard, same thing. Third guard, same thing. Finally he was in the courtroom and began to preach his famous sermon, "Prepare to meet thy God." He was well along when the court preacher stepped out. He wore a handmade silk shirt, some handmade Florsheim shoes and had a manicure. He was the court preacher. "Just a minute," he said, "I would like to suggest that perhaps you would do better if you went back to your own people. Go back and preach to the cows and the chickens. This is the king's court."

Amos never missed a beat. He said, "I was no prophet, neither was I a prophet's son; but I was an herdsman, and a gatherer of sycamore fruit: and the Lord took me as I followed the flock, and the Lord said unto me, 'Go, prophesy unto my people Israel.' Now, therefore, hear the word of the Lord." His authority was, "God told me to do this and I have to do it."

Priorities. Paul said, "None of these things moved me." He was under pressures, as all of us are. We feel a little sorry for ourselves. We get to thinking nobody ever had it like we have. Paul lived in a day when it was fatal to be found out as a Christian. There was little in the rights of a citizen, even as a Roman, that could protect one once he was discovered to be a Christian. Paul was under a lot of pressure. On his way to Jerusalem the Holy Spirit warned him in every city that he could expect bonds and imprisonment. He was walking straight into trouble and there were pressures from outside and pressures from the church and his own dear ones were weeping around him and saying, "What do you do this for? Don't walk into trouble. You don't have to do it that way. Be a little wise. Why do you want to get killed and be a memory? Why not live a little longer—bless a few more people!" He said, "None of these things move me, neither count I my life dear unto myself, so that I might finish my course with joy."

It is not what we are doing now that is so important, it is how it is going to end that counts! The priorities determine procedure. What we consider most important determines what we are going to do and, more importantly, how we are going to end. ". . .That I might finish my course with joy, and the ministry, which I have received of the Lord Jesus, to testify the gospel of the grace of God." Priorities determine which way we are moving and also whether or not we are getting the job done. We get busy doing a lot a things, things that keep us busy respectfully so that we do not have to grapple with the heartaches, the problems, the great principles that ought to be settled.

Show me a man who has decided the priorities in his life and is following those priorities and there will always be a few who will want to go along with him. We never lack for people to go along with us once we have decided what we must do under God. There went with Saul, when he was anointed as king, "a band of men whose hearts God had touched." David was in the cave of Adullam but he had a crowd that was willing to come and work with him by God's provision.

Get in Business with God

I am a little impatient with people who piously frown upon efficient methods for doing God's work. It is a little fashionable in some quarters to frown on anything that is too efficient in terms of handling God's money. We ought to get over that. This is, after all, the 20th-century and in every area of history the people God used were people who were sensible enough to use the means and the materials at hand.

Is there any reason why we should not talk in terms of

investment for the Lord? I had a conversation with a businessman who had gone through the wringer for about a year. He had overextended himself and had gone broke. In the process the Lord had spoken to his heart, humbled and revived him. Finally he found a businessman who was able and willing to bail him out for a slice of the business. Now he was doing very nicely, making more money personally than he had before and the business was doing better, at which point I said, "My brother, God has brought you through. What is your horizon now? What are you going to do now?"

"Well," he said, "I just hope to be able to buy this other fellow out so I will be able to own my business once again." I looked at him and said, "Why don't you make some plans about your business that are big enough for God to get in them? You're a nice guy and I love you, but you're a businessman, period. Why don't you operate your business for God? If you're going to make some money, why don't you make it for the Lord?" His eyes opened up and he looked at me and said, "I never thought of that."

We are the last great hope of missionary endeavor in the world. This is the only country in the world where one can give 50 per cent of his income to charitable and religious and educational causes and get deductions for it. Why not promote this new idea of taking some potential, whether money or stocks or a business or whatever, and investing it for God and operating it for God?

What does "all for Jesus" mean? It might mean that somebody who has a car dealership would start to operate it for the Lord. He will get his salary and above that his business will make some money. Out of the money it makes after the taxes are paid, why not see that the gospel is sent across the world?

Most Christians do not know what to do with their property. If they have a will it directs that after all just debts are paid, the remainder goes to the family. It is our duty as believers to provide for God's work in our wills, to take advantage of some of the tax shelters built into our system at this time. There will be less and less as the government gets hungrier and hungrier. But we do have them now. It is certainly not unspiritual to make a will that provides for the Lord's work.

Use Leisure Time for God

We need new insight for making our leisure time become productive for God. Why not take this idea of leisure time and make it start to pay for the Lord Jesus? We have heard of moonlighting. Has anybody ever suggested we might moonlight for the Lord?

If the Lord Jesus is everything we say he is and if a man can get away with a four-day week, is there anything wrong with his taking an extra job so he can support a missionary? The only thing that bothers us is that people are unwilling to do it because they want that money for themselves. So we get back to motivation again. The new leisure—make it profitable for the Lord. The only reason why a man's business should survive another few years is in order to get the gospel out across the world. Show me one person who is using his personal potential for the Lord and I will show you a number of people who get vaccinated with the idea, and it begins to bear fruit in their lives as well. The idea of getting the neighbors in for some coffee and coffee cake and study of the Word of God is catching fire all over the area in which I live. "Mrs. Jones" will invite some of her neighbors in on a Thursday morning for coffee. They come in and smoke their cigarettes and drink their coffee and eat their coffee cake. Then somebody opens up Romans. It is a new concept to some people that a person would actually open his house to the heathen without putting up a "no trespassing" sign. We would be surprised how much the kids would appreciate it if we volunteered our car to take them somewhere where they could hold a meeting to honor the Lord in some way and then buy them a little bit to eat on the way home so they could enjoy it that much more. We ought to use our car, our house, our personal potential for the Lord.

Investigate Personal Sacrifice

The power of personal sacrifice was dramatically illustrated in a meeting I held. Evon Hedley was with me at the time and remembers distinctly that when we got to town the chairman looked at us with dismay and said, "Oh, are you here already?" This was an ill omen and we soon found out the choir had not re-hearsed, the personal workers were not trained, all of the budget from preceding times had been spent and much of the advertising was still in somebody's backroom waiting to be distributed.

As the days went along we did have a good meeting with a lot of souls saved and we paid up. Here is how it happened. The chairman of the local committee got up one night and said, "I figure that if this thing is going to go, somebody has to really sacrifice and I've been praying about it and God told me I had to start it. I've been saving up some money— $100—so I could go on vacation. I have my $100 and I'm going to give it tonight." And he gave it. Some of the rest of God's people got behind it and we went out of town having seen the distinct blessing of God. It had to start with somebody saying, "I'm going to do it." Most of us do not really suffer very much by our sacrificing for the Lord's work.

Are your plans and your message big enough to challenge today's people? Every pastor knows the danger of allowing his board members to be bored by little stuff. He can always get an hour-and-a-half argument in any board meeting over who should have the keys to the church building, but when it comes to something important it does not take nearly as long. We allow people of real substance to be bored by little things, organizational junk. We are specialists in trivia and as a result we miss our own people. If we want stewardship, if we want people to follow us, we had better have something to say that is worthy of eternity. It is not enough to mouth the truisms. It is not enough to preach the truth. It is only enough when we preach it in the power of God and relate it to where people live. After we have said something from the Word of God somebody ought to be able to say, "Now I know what to do next Friday," in relation to some problem that he or she may be facing.

Cultivate a World Vision

Today's people think in terms of a whole world. They think in terms of rapid, worldwide travel, budgets in the billions and of whole nations being communicated with. They think in terms of things being done on a little higher scale, a little higher class than previously. The old days of three people standing on a street corner holding an open air meeting are largely over because if we want an open air meeting we had better have the kind people are used to having from the devil's crowd. The devil's crowd has open air meetings but they have pretty good music and well-dressed people and something equated with class in our day.

I do not say the gospel is not effective unless we dress it up. John the Baptist did not have a committee or a Hammond organ or a P.A. system. All he had was locusts and wild honey and the Holy Spirit. But John the Baptist lived in his day, and I wonder if he came today whether or not he would come with a girdle or camel's hair and eat locusts and wild honey. I doubt it.

We must be sure our message is dynamic enough and virile enough and godly enough to get a hearing with today's people. We must not be specialists in the tired cliche. When we have something to say that is worth listening to and have plans that are big enough for God and God's people to be challenged by them, then they will listen. In my experience people have never failed to rise to a challenge that had stature to it. I have been guilty of giving little challenges and getting little response. But whenever there was something which had the unavoidable ring of God's direction in it, the people rallied around it.

This is what stewardship is all about—my life on the line for Jesus Christ. We must decide what is worth dying for, then go to it and in the process do the very best and most efficient job we can, to communicate that challenge to as many people as we can while God gives us opportunity.

That does not mean, of course, that we have all the answers. The Christian has to face difficult questions. They are often the same questions people asked in Jesus' day.

10. Perplexing Questions and Providential Answers

Three questions asked of our Saviour and his disciples serve to point up quite accurately the areas which perplex the average human being until he walks with the King, Jesus Christ, for himself.

Christ Is Greater than Societal Barriers

The first question is found in Mark 2:16: "How is it that he eateth and drinketh with publicans and sinners?"

The background of this question is the fact that the Lord Jesus called as one of his disciples a man who was a tax collector. When our Lord asked Matthew to commit his life to him and become a disciple, one of the first things that happened was that Matthew got all his friends and buddies together so they also might meet the Master. Of course, the people in the circle in which he moved were something like himself—they also were corrupt politicians, and people whom the Bible calls "sinners." This includes folk whose life style was publicly out of line with the law of God: the drunk, the prostitute, the petty thief, the pickpocket—you name it . . . sinners. Matthew started where he was, with people he knew, and shared his faith in Jesus with them.

Now came the question: "How is it," his opponents said, "that he eateth and drinketh with publicans (that includes grafters and crooks and corrupt politicians) and sinners (that's everything from the pick-pocket to the prostitute and back again, including a few drunks)?" In other words, they complained that our Lord was mixing socially with people who were beneath him.

79

It is the barriers between people that seem to form the structure of most societies! The moment you break down the barriers—*really* break them down—you are threatening the identity of those whose only mark of distinction is their refusal to meet on a basis of equality with those they consider beneath them.

And yet this is precisely the point at which the Lord Jesus Christ makes a difference in one's life. Some time ago, we had a student at The King's College who was from the Arab side of the world. He is a beautiful person, who truly knows and loves the Lord Jesus Christ as his Saviour. His life was a constant, living proof that Christ is real. He went to a student conference which was attended by thousands of college students from many countries of the world. On the platform along with this young man was an Israeli who also had trusted Christ as his Messiah. There they sat, side by side, on the platform. When it came time for our young student to speak, he said, "One of the most wonderful things about being a Christian is that because our Lord Jesus has put his love in my heart, I now have love for my brother from Israel." And the two of them stood there with their arms about each other's shoulders, the tears of joy running down their faces—living proof that God breaks down man-made barriers.

Helpful legislation is all well and good, and some of it is long overdue. But you do not, in the long run, change society by legislation. Society is changed by the dynamics of an inner revolution. Society can only be changed when man's heart is changed. "Out of the heart," said Solomon, "are the issues of life."

They Need Me

The Master had a simple and direct answer to the question, "Why is he eating with people whom we consider beneath us?" His answer was, "They need me . . . they need me!" The key word here is *need*. "They that are well have no *need* of a physician, but they that are sick. I came not to call the righteous but sinners to repentance." Your reason for contacting people is that they need your Lord. If you remember that, it will make a difference in your relationship with others, automatically.

Talking with people, overcoming social barriers, mixing with those who are not in your station of life, going beyond your own tight little circle of friends . . . the reason is very simple: They need you, because they need the Lord Jesus Christ!

Somebody needs you today! Forget the man-made barriers that divide people. Find that someone, and introduce him to your Saviour!

Christ Provides the Extra, External Dimension to Living

The second question asked of our Lord had to do with the disciples' lack of observing routine religious customs such as fasting on certain days of the week. Mark 2:18 says that the people asked, "Why do the disciples of John and of the Pharisees fast, but thy disciples fast not?"

Just as secular society is often built upon barriers which divide people, so religious society is often built upon ritual observances which soothe and give status to people. Fasting was one such observance. A good Pharisee would deprive himself of food for certain hours on two or even three days each week, thereby gaining status in the eyes of his fellow-men, and assuring himself that he was, indeed, a very holy person!

The problem is, of course, that nothing you can *do* will ever provide the extra dimension of life and freedom to your daily existence.

Christ's answer was disarmingly simple: "Man," he exclaimed, "you don't fast when you go to a wedding reception, do you? I'm here, and for my disciples, life is a continual feast of good things. They may not have much, but they have me!"

Using the twin figures of speech of new wine in old

wineskins, and new, unshrunk cloth sewed upon an old
garment, he taught again the truth: Christ is the new dimension in living . . . greater than the old observances which
serve merely as a crutch for one's self-esteem . . . greater than
the old wineskins of past enjoyments and achievement . . .
greater than the old fabric of belief and custom! The great
secret, says Paul, is "Christ in you, the hope of glory!"

In our day, people are talking about being "turned off' by
the church. What they really are saying is that institutionalized religion with its many forms and customs seems to be
existing by and for itself, rather than as an evidence of the
presence of God. And so, the question asked in the days of
our Lord Jesus is quite appropriate for today. Is a real experience with Christ so great that it just won't be contained by
institutionalized religion? In other words, if I become a New
Testament Christian, am I going to forsake the church? Is the
church dead? Is it all gone?

No, not that. I think the question goes deeper than that.
The presence of the Lord Jesus Christ creates a dynamic
power within the individual which is greater than any kind
of religious regimentation. Now this does not mean that you
are going to "forsake the assembling of yourselves together
as the manner of some is." We ought to go to church. We
ought to fellowship with other believers—the Bible teaches
that. But it also teaches that Jesus is greater than religious
custom. He is the new, eternal dimension to living.

David points out in Psalm 24 that the prime requisite for
religion that is acceptable with God is a clean life and a pure
heart. God requires a life that is right on the inside. The only
way to achieve that is through faith in the Lord Jesus. Commit yourself completely to him and allow him, by his Holy
Spirit working in your life, to change you from what you
were, to what he wants you to be. 2 Corinthians 5:17 says it:
"If any man be in Christ, he is a new creature . . . ." God
demands a new creation, not an old custom!

You might ask, "Why should I put myself out at all, or
give up anything in the name of my religious faith? Why

should I ever fast, for instance, give up a meal and use the time in praying instead?"

I think fasting is helpful from the purely human point of view: it helps to focus your attention on God. If you do give up your lunch or dinner or all three meals for one day, you will be powerfully hungry before the day has gone on very far. The pangs of hunger remind you that you are doing something different from your normal routine. That reminds you: Why am I hungry? I am hungry because I am especially seeking God today. So you go on with your praying, and you are enabled to seek God throughout the whole day.

Use fasting as a means of breaking through the crust of your own soul, in faith and in obedience. Remember, God wants a life that is right with him and man, more than he wants anything you can do by way of fasting and prayer. A changed life—that's it! There just isn't room for the new wine in the old wineskins.

Today, with a wholly reckless abandon, turn yourself over to the Lord and let him begin to work in and through, and beyond, and in spite of religious routines. God is greater than any routine you will ever establish. Therein lies the answer Jesus gave when they asked why his disciples didn't observe the customs of institutionalized religion. The answer was, "Jesus is greater than the customs!" He, and he alone, provides the extra dimension of eternity to everyday life. "Christ liveth in me," declared Paul, "and the life which I now live in the flesh I live by the faith of the Son of God."

Lord of All

The third question that was asked of our Lord Jesus Christ is found in Mark 2:24. The Pharisees asked, "Why do they (the disciples) on the sabbath day that which is not lawful?"

In those days, the paths which led from one village to another frequently wound their way through grain fields.

When the harvest was ripe, it was quite permissible for the passerby to help himself to a few handfuls of grain, rub the kernels briskly between his palms, blow away the chaff, and have a nourishing morsel of food to hold him over until lunch time! This was the process used by the disciples as they walked along the way one sabbath day. What they were doing was perfectly legal, but technically, it was considered by the Pharisees to be threshing grain, and threshing was work. The law of Moses says no work on the sabbath; ergo, the disciples were disobeying the Mosaic law.

Our Saviour did not argue this point, except to point out that King David, in an instance of extreme need, had dined on the shewbread, something reserved exclusively for the priests. In effect, our Lord said, the sabbath was given to provide rest and worship for man, not to bind him with petty rules.

The entire conversation turns, however, on our Lord's comment as found in the last verse of Mark 2: "The Son of man is Lord also of the sabbath."

Lord *also*? Also what?

Look at the second chapter of Mark from the point of view of Christ's Lordship, and see this question of adherence to religious rules in true perspective.

It is Christ's Lordship that makes all the difference!

In Mark 2:5, he is Lord of forgiven sin!

In verse 11, he is Lord of renewed strength and health!

In verse 14, he is Lord of a changed life!

In verses 18 to 22, he is Lord of fulfillment and joy!

In the same passage, he is Lord of new dimensions in living!

And of course, in the passage on the sabbath, he is Lord of new perspective.

Make Christ truly Lord of your life, and you'll find these blessed truths come trooping down from the Throne of Grace to find lodgement in your heart and in your daily life!

Make him Lord of all!

The problem most of us face is that we are quite willing to

profess a complete surrender to our Lord in matters that are religious; but in non-religious, secular, everyday matters, we insist on making our own decisions. Will we ever learn? It is in the small, non-religious matters of daily life that a person's destiny is determined.

Learn today the meaning of "Lord also . . ." Let him be Lord of your career, your business, your education, your home, your children, your budget, your lifestyle, your recreation and your leisure . . . Lord of all!

I promise you: Small things, petty things, and the everyday burdens each of us bear—none of these will ever be able to put you into bondage when you make Christ Lord of all of your life! When he is Lord, you can begin to experience the joy of really *living* Colossians 3:23: "And whatsoever ye do, do it heartily, as to the Lord, and not unto men; knowing that of the Lord ye shall receive the reward of the inheritance: for ye serve the Lord Christ."

That's living life with real zest!

11. New Zest for Living

Ask yourself:
>   . . .Is my spiritual life at a standstill?
>   . . .Do I really want to get off dead center?
>   . . .Do I look for something to rid me of
>   dragging inertia?

If your answer is "Yes," then Psalm 119 has some great answers! Look at verses 25 to 32:

> My soul cleaveth unto the dust:
> quicken thou me according to thy word.

> I have declared my ways, and
> thou heardest me: teach me thy statutes.

> Make me to understand the way of thy precepts:
> so shall I talk of thy wondrous works.

> My soul melteth for heaviness:
> strengthen me according unto thy word.

> Remove from me the way of lying:
> and grant me thy law graciously.

> I have chosen the way of truth:
> Thy judgments have I laid before me.

> I have stuck unto thy testimonies:
> O Lord, put me not to shame.

> I will run the way of thy commandments,
> when thou shalt enlarge my heart.

This passage highlights two problems, well-known to each of us: one—the difficulty of getting started at what we know we ought to do. And two—the failure to follow through.

Many of us are good beginners but poor finishers. About the middle of any given assignment we tend to sag a little. Have you found that true of you? We offer all kinds of alibis. We say, "I don't think I can do this. I'll turn it over to Joe Schmoe, and let him take care of it." Or we run out of steam in the middle of some task and fail to follow through.

I Must Admit I Need Fixing

"My soul cleaveth unto the dust: quicken thou me according to thy word" (v. 25).

What does the phrase "cleaveth unto the dust" mean? Quite simply, it means I stick to what I'm made of. We are human beings, made of human clay. We share human faults and foibles. We tend to gravitate to the lowest level.

One of the great proofs of the fallacy of the naturalistic theory of evolution is that, although it assumes that man, left to himself, will evolve upward, the very proof tests show that he does not. The proponents of this theory teach that every kind of life, including man, will improve by the law which they term "natural selection." But this is not true in nature.

Have you had a baked potato lately, an Idaho potato? You may or may not know it is a hybrid plant, brought to its present state through years of breeding by experts in agriculture.

Suppose you take an Idaho potato, cut it up and plant the portions that have eyes in them, and then go away and do nothing for a period of years. What will you get? Well, you'll get the equivalent of what Bob Hope talked about describing *his* potato crop. He said some were as large as golf balls and some were as large as peas, and there were quite a few small ones.

Likewise you leave people to themselves—without the

operation of the grace of God in their lives—and their spiritual life will deteriorate.

The Psalmist says, "My soul cleaveth unto the dust." The only way to improve youself is to give yourself to the Improver. He made you, so he knows how to deal with you, all for good. That's good news for me!

You remember the story of the young man who was driving a Model T Ford. Some sort of mechanical breakdown occurred. The driver was completely dismayed because he didn't know how to get the car started.

The story goes that a long black touring car came alongside this defunct machine, and a tall, thin, cadaverous-looking gentleman got out.

He went over to the car and said, "What's the matter, Bud?"

"Mister, this thing won't go."

"Well, let me take a look at it." So the stranger twisted this and adjusted that and then he said, "Now turn the motor over and let's see what happens."•

So the boy turned the key—the old Fords used to have four separate coils that would buzz, do you remember that? When you turned the key on it would go buzz-z-z-z, and then you pressed the starter and the motor leaped into life. The young man did as instructed. Oh, what a lovely sound a Model T made when it was running right! It was a combination of asthma and the Fourth of July—sort of an explosive cough.

So there it was, running, and the boy was so happy. "Mister," he said, "I'd like to thank you. What is your name?"

(You've seen it coming, haven't you?) The stranger said, "I'm Henry Ford." He knew all about Model T's because he made them.

My friend, God made you. He's the only one who can fix you and get you going. But he *can*. The Psalmist said in effect, "I've got an affinity for the wrong thing. I need fixing and the only way for this to be accomplished is for Someone to give me new *life*. Quicken me," he said, "according to thy word."

I Must Submit My
Habit Patterns to God

Generally speaking, we keep on operating very much the same way day after day. Often our habit patterns are established along the line of mediocrity and self-will. Now *mediocrity* is being the best of the lousiest and the lousiest of the best, as Paul Harvey says. And *self-will* is pretty plain to all of us—"I want what I want when I want it," as Harry Lawder used to sing. Well, you put those together and you have predictable trouble.

How do I change my habit patterns? The only way is by substituting something good for something harmful—and I cannot do this myself. But *God* does it for each of us when we turn our lives over to him and let him direct our actions, our thoughts and our motives—all in line with his truth and his will.

Prompt and positive obedience to the Word of God on my part will work wonders. The process isn't complex. I don't have to make a federal case of it. I just decide to *obey God* rather than to seek my own good and at once, and continually, he gives me the energy and directives that I need.

I Must Be Open to Change

Most of us like things pretty much just as they are. Husbands dislike having furniture rearranged. Wives complain about altered schedules. It's hard to get an employee to adopt new procedures.

Have you people in management tried to put in a new system recently? You probably encountered resistance. In all probability your colleagues weren't against you as manager. Nor were they necessarily against the new system which, it could be argued, was much better than the present one. They were just against change, period.

From a spiritual viewpoint, once you've realized the fact that human nature always clings to the present and the familiar, once you admit that you don't *like* to change your ways but that *God* can deal with you gently, understandingly, all the pain goes out of the process! It isn't a traumatic experience. If you let him, God can modify your conduct, without breaking your back or breaking your heart. Hallelujah!

As an aside here, and by way of illustration, let's think about "changes" that have died aborning though they have been submitted to committees composed of able and well-intentioned men and women. Here's a tip worth repeating, which you may want to use some time: If you want action, you don't bring up anything frontally to a committee and ask the members to vote on it promptly, for if you do, the result will usually be a resounding "No."

If we're honest with ourselves, we don't like change. But God does not expect any one of us to change himself. He will do the changing if I will do the committing.

I Must Verbalize Specific Confession

"I have declared my ways, and thou heardest me: teach me thy statutes" (v. 26).

I must learn the value of verbalized, specific confession to God, not only as a penitent but also as a learner. It's awfully hard to tell God the truth. Most of us make little bland speeches to him; Lord, bless this and bless that; thank you for this and thank you for that, and so on. It's very difficult for us to confess something specific that needs changing.

When I am in charge of an extended prayer meeting (some all night), I always follow this plan. After a few hours of intercession, say about one or two o'clock in the morning, I give this invitation: "Who is there here who isn't right with the Lord but wants to be? At this point, let's not pray for other people. Let's use the personal pronoun, 'Lord, this is what I need.'" That's a fruitful kind of praying.

I recall that on one occasion in São Paulo, Brazil, we were

having an all-night prayer meeting and at one point I urged that we should all be honest with God—not make a speech to him, but tell him the truth, each for himself.

Then I heard an agonized voice from *under* the grand piano from a brother who was on his hands and knees, crying out to God. In essence this was his prayer: "O God, I've been dishonest all through my college and seminary days. I didn't get my degrees honestly. I cheated on my exams. I'm a defeated man. I don't want to go back to the United States defeated. Please help me."

Well, that man got through to God as you can well imagine he would! When he came home he wrote to the president of his college and laid the matter fully and honestly before him. This young man said he had gotten right with God and he wanted to make things right with his school. He sent me a carbon copy of the letter. Here was personal, verbalized, specific confession to God that had an appeal also to those he had wronged.

Some of you men, and ladies too, have been in management of different kinds through the years. You know this is true: When an employee makes a mistake, you don't go to him or her and pound that one over the head and say, "What did you do that for!"

You don't do that if you want to develop the employee. Rather, you say, "Now the next time, I'd like you to do it this way, because I think you'll find it will work better." That's called management by expectation, management by results, management by goals.

So here we are with you as the "employee," the learner. Let the blessed Holy Spirit say to you, "Now next time this happens (whatever it is), do it this way: Let *me* guide you."

What a delight it is to learn from God that way! He doesn't give up on you on any given Wednesday morning—or ever.

Have you ever really talked over your faults with Jesus? Have you said, "Lord, my trouble is I have a quick temper"? "Lord, I have such a sharp tongue"? "Lord, my trouble is I'm unforgiving; I hold grudges"? "Lord, I'm greedy .... I'm always late .... I tend to trim the truth when I'm under pressure"? Are you in the habit of telling God the truth about yourself?

As you particularize your situation, you take the position not only of a penitent asking for pardon but also of a listener asking for direction. And oh, how he loves to teach us, doesn't he?

"Take my yoke upon you," said he. And what's the next word? "Learn of me." The Pennsylvania Dutch have a saying, "Ve git too soon oldt und too late schmart." I hope I can really *learn* from him before I get too old to have it do me any good.

It's wonderful to talk over our needs and our frailties and our faults with God and then hear him say, "Yes, I know. Now next time do it *this* way, my way."

I Must See the Gospel in Relation to Everday Life

"Make me to understand the way of thy precepts; so shall I talk of thy wondrous works" (v. 27).

What the Psalmist is saying is this: Understanding of and witness to "the way" go together. There is a remarkable relation between improved motivation on my part—in other words, I get going—and improved understanding of how the gospel works. I can't tell you *why* this is so. I only know that it is. In other words, if you want a life that is improved in *all* its aspects, then improve your performance at the gospel level.

For example, you pray with somebody for salvation, and I'll guarantee that you won't hate to do the dishes quite so much as before you prayed. You won't put off cleaning the garage quite so long. You won't procrastinate about answering your mail quite so much. There is a stimulating factor associated with winning somebody to Christ that improves all the other aspects of one's life. Of course, you have to take this pronouncement by faith, because until you try this principle you won't know that it works. But *do* it!

Returning to the business world for another illustration, let us say you have a salesman who habitually gets to work late. He takes long coffee breaks. He enjoys two-hour lunches. He quits work early. He isn't producing. In a word, nothing is going right for or with him.

In a situation like this you can do one of two things. Either you can fire the man or you can improve him. If you don't want to fire him, how do you go about improving him?

You say, "John, I want you to come with me on some calls today. I need your help."

You have already lined up some calls where you know orders will be given automatically, for the prospects need these items and are ready to buy them. They're going to order, say, three dozen desks at $560 apiece and a dozen filing cabinets and other gorgeous expensive things that you love to see listed on your order pad.

So you take this defeated empolyee with you—this poor "dedicated clod"—a candidate for dismissal.

As you make the calls, you lead him into saying something about the product. Then the sale is closed and he sees with delight that the order is being written up (and you've already told him you are going to split the commission with him).

I'll guarantee that man will be at work earlier the next day and will have new zest for his job. He will have his prospect cards laid out. He will ring more doorbells. Why? Because he has had an experience of success in selling his product.

That's business. It's done every day. Any book on sales training will have a chapter on how to do the very thing I have described.

Now bring the matter into the spiritual realm. While you might never call yourself a clod, or allow anybody else to use that word as applied to you, you are fully aware that you are unproductive, lacking enthusiasm, drive and carry-through. The Word of God contains all the directives you need for improvement.

If you want to modify your conduct to the point where

you are motivated to do the will of God—do it eagerly, effectively and promptly—then specialize in "selling the product" which is the gospel, in leading people to Jesus Christ. That vitality will not only make you a soul-winner but it will also filter into every other area of your life, with blessed results.

I Must Rely on God's Strength

Having dealt with the question of one's getting started in the first place in this matter of living and witnessing for Christ, we now look at the problem of follow-through.

"My soul melteth for heaviness; strengthen thou me according unto thy word" (v. 28).

The only way to carry on God's work to completion is by appropriating *his* strength. Some of you know this truth much better than I. You've been through the battles of life and you're a little ahead of me in learning this process. Many times you have had to say, "O God, strengthen me now to go through this"—and he did, didn't he? Each of us gets real strength to go through the hard things of life not from good advice nor from the fellowship we enjoy with each other—valuable as these are—but from the impact of the Word of God upon our hearts.

Jesus said, "The words that I speak unto you, they are spirit, and they are *life*" (John 6:63).

The writer to the Hebrews declares, "The word of God is quick, and powerful, and sharper than any two-edged sword . . ." (Hebrews 4:12). "Quick" means alive—the Word of God is alive and full of power. It exerts a tremendous influence—in discernment, in enabling—on the one who lives by it.

The Word *cleanses*—the washing of water by the Word.

The Word *brings faith*—faith cometh by hearing and hearing by the Word of God.

The Word *leads to prayer*—wait on the Lord and he shall strengthen thine heart.

The Word *interprets suffering,* as being itself a kind of

strength. You may have the marks of suffering on you. But, under God, you may become a stronger and abler and more worthwhile person.

For an illustration of how the Word of God brings strength, look at Ezra 7:10: "Ezra had prepared his heart to seek the law of the Lord, and to do it"—that means not only to hear but also to obey, "*do* it."

What happened? Verse 28 tells us: "I was *strengthened* as the hand of the Lord my God was upon me."

Yes, you can get strength as you wait upon God. This means not just praying, not just reading the Bible, but a combination of these two plus a willingness—even an eagerness—for God to apply the Word to the weak points in your life. It's a daily process. You won't "sag" in the middle of some assignment if you learn the secret of going to God and letting him give you the strength you need when you need it—*his* strength.

I Must Be Honest

"Remove from me the way of lying" (v. 29).

There is a weakening process involved in any inconsistency or dishonesty on my part. I must face the fact that anything I try to cover up will weaken me somewhere along the line.

You and I are faulty human beings; there's not a perfect person in the crowd. While we readily admit that fact, we have to face up to this principle: Absolute honesty with God produces the ability to go on with God. Make a habit of leveling with God about yourself when you pray. You will find that as a result he will give you his enablement in glorious ways.

Sin is a deterrent to learning. If I want the Bible to come alive for me—if I want to learn something from it—I must honestly admit, "Yes, Lord, that's me," when I am faced with its correctives.

Sin is a deterrent to production. Here is a man who was doing a pretty good job, let us say, on an assembly line. All of

Walk With the King Today

a sudden there is a fantastic rise in his spoilage rate. In other words, too large a number of the widgets that are turned out won't pass inspection. His whole performance is off. There may be a number of factors to produce this result. But in all probability there is some big, personal heart need that is keeping him from doing a good job.

Sin is a deterrent to good interpersonal relations. All of us have had the experience of meeting somebody who, for no apparent good reason, fairly bit our heads off. Later we may have found that that person was under deep conviction. God was dealing with him or her and the reaction was for that person to fight back.

"Remove from me the way of lying." Is this an exercise for *Christians*? Paul warned the Colossians (3:9): "Lie not one to another." On the positive side, he enjoined believers to be "speaking the truth in love" (Ephesians 4:15). If there is disharmony in my own church, I ought to look for two things: Am I being absolutely honest about myself (not prideful, not boasting)? And am I being perceptive and honest about my brother (about his abilities, his needs, and his importance in the Body of Christ)?

I Must Recognize the Relation of My Mind to My Conduct

"I have chosen the way of truth: thy judgments have I laid before me" (v. 30).

This statement, "I have chosen the way of truth," is in opposition to verse 9, "Remove from me the way of lying." Now the psalmist says *I* have *chosen* something. In other words, your mind determines what you are going to do and say. ("As a man thinketh in his heart, so is he.") Commitment to the Word of God and the will of God is absolutely essential to any improvement in my performance.

Many of you who read these lines have been serving the Lord Jesus for years. So for me to say to you, "You have to choose Christ" is tautology; it's repeating the same thing, like saying "green grass is green."

But there is another sense in which choosing is vital, and

it concerns the hundred or so little decisions that make up each day. The way to improve my living is to say at each decision point, "Lord, I choose *your* way."

Look at this principle from a spiritual point of view. What is on your *mind* will be reflected in your *conduct*. That is what the psalmist says: "Thy testimonies (judgments) have I laid before me." So put the Word of God into your mind. Pick a verse every day and go over it through the day, "chewing" on it, savoring its delicious taste. You will find that the *Word* affects your *work*. It will change you, strengthen, sweeten you, in all the areas of your life.

I Must Keep on Keeping On

"I will run in the way of thy commandments, when thou shalt enlarge my heart" (v. 32).

The *Pilgrim Bible* comments: "When the affection or love of the heart is aroused for the Word, its commandments will be obeyed."

Persistence is directly related to an enlarged capacity for God. Some people are 22-caliber souls. They are little pea shooters. They lack capacity because they have never developed an outreach for God. Once they've gotten past the 23rd Psalm and the Lord's Prayer (by reading and application), they are out of their depth entirely.

But it is gloriously possible to have an enlarged—and enlarging—capacity for God. That comes from meditating upon his Word and doing his will. Make a bigger place for God in your soul and you'll have greater evidence of God in your conduct. The enlarging is the outcome of the persistent practice of opening one's life to the Word. How is this to be done?

At this point I would like to share with you a couple of "small thoughts," as I call them, not directly related to the passage we have been considering, but offering practical suggestions.

If you want the Lord to "enlarge your heart"—to increase your capacity to love and serve him, do this:

First, "prioritize" the things you need to do. You know what a priority is: something that must be done first, because it is of first importance. All right, make a list of all the things you need to do and align them in the order of their importance. Then as you begin the day, do the most important one first, and on down the line. If you miss a few at the bottom, that doesn't matter. And if your carefully-worked-out schedule is interrupted, don't worry—God uses interruptions. But at the end of the day you still will have the solid satisfaction of having done the things that mattered.

This is a procedure that many believers don't know anything about. It will make your days meaningful and it will keep you from being frustrated by half-failure. In other words, it will "enlarge" your capacity for learning and doing.

By all means do this "prioritizing" before bedtime, for the simple reason that you have a "computer" between your ears—your unconscious mind—and when you feed into it the list you have prepared and when you pray over it and then lay it aside, your unconscious mind will work on it helpfully all night long. You will wake up with a clear awareness of how to proceed. Do the most important thing first, because it is probably the hardest.

Second, try a "dry run." Do you know what we mean by a "dry run"? It is a procedure you employ to see whether it will work, without necessarily risking a situation on it.

I took part in a telecast panel discussion recently. When we were all properly made up for the cameras the director said, "Now we'll do a dry run."

"A what?" I wanted to know.

"We'll do the program exactly as if you were on the air—only you won't be, yet."

So we talked to each other and the panel went on. "Fine," the director said, "now we'll record it."

Form the habit of doing a "dry run" on something that has been scaring you to death or that you have been putting off doing because it is difficult. In other words, say to yourself. *"If* I were to do this, how would I proceed?"

You're not risking anything. Nobody's watching you. If the idea doesn't work, nobody's going to blame you. You're just "trying it on for size."

Businessmen call this action a planning procedure. By means of computers they schedule an entire job in advance, paying special attention to all the things that could possibly go wrong. (You know Murphy's Law: If anything can go wrong, it will.)

Now you take the task that is troubling you. Look at it and say, "*If* I were to do it, how would I begin?"

Did you ever have a difficult letter to write, and you put off writing it? You said, "Oh, I just can't get at it."

I have to write advertising and promotional copy and I'm often the chief bottleneck at that point in our organization. I love to write, but I don't get at it. So I see the deadline coming closer and closer. I look at the job that is required of me and I say, "Oh man, I've got to get at this, but it's hard!" (How can you be inspired on signal?)

But then I put a piece of paper in the typewriter and I say, "Now, Cook, if you were going to do this (but you *aren't*, of course, because you *can't*), what would you say?"

Before long my brain gets out of creeper gear and into overdrive and the copy has been written.

These are workable suggestions; I know, for I use them. But they must be persistently followed if they are to be tools in God's hands to "enlarge" your heart and your ministry.

The Final Question

Do I really *want* new zest for living? Do I *want* to get off dead center? Do I *want* to be rid of the inertia that is ruining my life and my service?

The answer is clear: "Delight thyself also in the Lord; and he shall give thee the desires of thine heart. Commit thy way unto the Lord; trust also in him; and he shall bring it to pass (that is, he worketh)." (Psalm 37:4,5).

With that new zest for living, you're now ready for some real mind-changing thoughts!

12. Great Thoughts that Will Change Your Life

What is the greatest thought you have ever had?

If you have never asked yourself that question, try it. You may be amazed and challenged and inspired.

Obviously, our "great thoughts," if they could all be set down, would show how different we are one from another. But from the long list that would emerge at least seven tremendous concepts would stand out. Let's look at them.

Form Versus Reality

There is a vast difference between form and reality. Our Lord Jesus Christ clearly indicates that it is possible for one to be ecclesiastically correct—to preach, to work miracles, to be successfully busy in the name of the Lord—and still be lost. These are his words, not mine:

> "Not every one that saith unto me, Lord, Lord, shall enter into the kingdom of heaven
> . . . .
> Many will say to me in that day, Lord, Lord, have we not prophesied in thy name? and in thy name have cast out devils? and in thy name done many wonderful works? And then I will profess unto them, I never knew you . . ." (Matthew 7:21-23).

The apostle Paul stresses the same truth in 2 Timothy 3:5 where he speaks of those who have a "form of godliness" but who lack the power thereof.

This difference between form and reality is no idle subject. Nor is it just a beginning point for a sermon that is to go on. It is as important to each of us as a jugular vein. The Bible says that if you have the Son of God, you have life—that is reality. And if you do not have the Son as your Saviour, your
100

teacher, your guide, everything else is meaningless form. It is dreadfully possible to be sitting in church, looking alive, but actually to be a spiritual corpse.

I ask you: Do you really *know* him? Is he your Lord? Does he bless you and walk with you and guide you? Do you have the assurance from the Holy Spirit's presence within that you are God's child? This is what counts. Not dead othodoxy but living truth. Not busy work but the miracle of the power of God working in you.

One of the things I have to continually impress upon the young people at The King's College is that to be a genuine Christian means to let the Lord Jesus into the total life, even non-religious affairs. The Lord Jesus has to be real when the clothesline breaks . . . when you have a blowout on the way to a wedding . . . when you forget to add the baking powder to the cake and it turns out to be a lovely flop just when Mrs. Gadabout is coming for tea—and she will tell the whole neighborhood what a poor cook you are.

Jesus Christ has to be real when there is too much month left over at the end of the money . . . when you think you have the juicy contract landed and then the phone rings and you hear, "Sorry, we won't be able to go through with it"—and you have already bought the raw material for the job.

The Lord Jesus Christ has to be real when you become the butt of somebody's unwarranted blame. You didn't deserve it and there is no way to answer it. You seethe and burn inwardly when some one has lied about you or criticized you unjustly. Christ has to be real where you live and when and where you hurt. And bless God, if he is real there, nothing else matters. Hallelujah! This is a great thought. It is foundational. Everything else of value stems from it. Now look at a second "great thought."

Redirected Focus

It is possible to change the focus of your life from yourself to others.

Several years ago I was present at a Youth for Christ

Congress in Japan. There were delegates from all over the world, with quite a few from North America. During the Congress, many of our North American friends gave a word of testimony by interpretation. I listened to the Japanese translation of these messages, and since I already knew the English, I paid attention to the Japanese equivalent to see if I could make out the foreign words. There was one expression that kept being repeated. It intrigued me so much that I finally went to the interpreter and asked what this word was. I found it was the personal pronoun "I." These dear people were talking more about themselves than anything else! However, as the week wore on, and God got through to some folks, we heard less and less of the personal pronoun and more and more of words pointing to the Lord Jesus Christ.

We are all self-centered. (Whose face do you look for in a group picture?) All of us are like the disciples to whom Jesus said, "Lift up your eyes and look on the fields." He said that to people who were interested in lunch. It was as though they had canvassed all the delicatessens and had finally found one that sold delicious corned beef and all the rest of those kosher delicacies. They came back and spread out the lunch and said, "Master, eat."

He told them, "I have meat to eat that ye know not of." They immediately resented his words and his attitude and said in effect, "Isn't that a nerve! Here we were walking our feet to the bone, trying to find someone whose store was open at noon when every respectable person is taking his siesta. We finally found food and brought it here and now he says he isn't hungry!" And they were put out about it.

In our way of speaking the Lord replied, "Fellas, you've got your eyes on the wrong thing. You're looking for groceries instead of looking for souls. Lift up your eyes and look on the fields for they are white already to harvest."

At just that moment a sizeable group of men came out from the town because the Samaritan woman (formerly a hussy) had been there, being a missionary. It was she who got this congregation together.

And Jesus said to the disciples, *"There's* the harvest, fellas. Get your eyes on people, not on provender. Get your eyes on souls, not symptoms. Get your eyes on others' needs, not on your own little troubles."

You say, "Now wait a minute. You used the word 'little.'" Sure, it's scriptural. "Our light affliction, which is but for a moment, worketh for us a far more exceeding and eternal weight of glory" (2 Corinthians 4:17).

The "great thought" in all this is that you can, by the grace of God, change the focus of your life, and he will bless you and bless others when you do this.

Activist for Christ

It is possible to become a Christian activist. The radicals have stolen that word and smeared it. But it is a good word: activist. It means to do something wholesome and constructive about a situation. Last week somebody sent me a beautiful motto. It says, "DO something: Lead, Follow, or Get Out of the Way." It is surprising that a small amount of doing can solve many problems.

There is always something you can do in any situation. Let me illustrate that point. In Judges 7:21 we find Gideon with 300 people in his army. Thirty thousand men had been sent home: 20,000 were scared and the other 10,000 were careless. All that were left were 300 men. They had the equivalent of an Ever-Ready flashlight, a cornet and a water pitcher. The Bible says "They stood every man in his place round about the camp; and all the host ran, and cried, and fled"—scared to death. "Every man"—there's no substitute for personal responsibility. Each of us has his separate job to perform. We can perform it best if we have learned the secret of trusting God actively throughout the day.

Greet your Lord in the morning. Pray before you have breakfast. Pray before you tackle your first job of the day,

whether in the home, the office, the schoolroom or whatever. Pray before you open a letter—it might be a check for
$5,000 or a bill for that much. Those of us on the radio know
it might be a scathing anonymous letter signed "A dear
friend in Christ."

Yes, *do* something: pray. In other words, become a Christian activist by praying first and then following through on
what the Lord says to you. If you will do this, God, through
the Holy Spirit, will enable you to do something glorious this
year. That is a great thought.

The Price of Leadership

Another great thought is that *leadership is possible, and that
it is costly.* Paul said to Timothy, "The things that thou hast
heard of me among many witnesses, the same commit thou
to *faithful* men, who shall be able to teach others also" (2
Timothy 2:2). "It is required in stewards, that a man be found
faithful" (1 Corinthians 4:2). Are you faithful? If you are always
late for Sunday School or not there at all, you are saying to
those who are watching you that it isn't all that important. If
as a teacher you are unprepared, if you drone through the
lesson, you are saying that the Word of God doesn't mean
much to you. Are you prompt or chronically late? Do you
give up when the going is hard and the responsibility gall-
ing? Faithfulness is the price of leadership. It is a great
thought that God, through the Holy Spirit, can *make* you
faithful (if you want him to): "The fruit of the Spirit is . . .
faith (faithfulness)" (Galatians 5:22).

The Contemporary and the Worldly

There is a difference between contemporaneity and worldliness.
I tell the young people at The King's College that the Lord
wants us to be sharp. I don't think there is any good purpose
served by looking either freakish or old-fashioned. Some
people think you have to be weird to be with it.

When we say "world" we don't mean the world of trees
and flowers and mountains and lakes that God made beautiful. We are talking about the world system that bypasses

God—the Garden of Eden philosophy brought up to date. "Cheat a little," it says; "it's good for you." . . . "Nice guys finish last, so don't mind who it is that you climb over, or how—just get to the top." . . . "Give yourself a break; you only live once and are a long time dead, so live it up—have a blast." . . . "Don't get too religious; you will lose friends, careers and money." . . . "Prayer is all right, but don't be radical about it." . . . "Be your own guy and run your own life."

That's worldliness. It cannot be defined by means of any list of "don'ts" that we ordinarily associate with our fundamentalism.

Mind you, I am a fundamentalist—I use the word benignly. I hold to the fundamentals of the Christian faith. I believe the whole Word of God and I'm going to continue to stand on it and preach it. But by the same token, I know that worldliness has gotten into the heart of many a person whose doctrine is impeccable and whose conduct cannot be criticized. It can get into my heart—or yours. It is the love of money or ease or position or any one of a score of other things that take over the rulership of the life. And remember: "All that is in the world (the world system), the lust of the flesh, and the lust of the eyes, and the pride of life, is not of the Father . . . And the world passeth away, and the lust thereof: but he that doeth the will of God abideth forever" (1 John 2:16, 17). "Whosoever therefore will be a friend of the world is the enemy of God" (James 4:4). Those are strong words. There is no grey there. It is clear black and white. What a great—and sobering—thought it is that there is a difference between the contemporary and the worldly.

Informality and Carelessness
There is a difference between informality and carelessness. In this day we don't stand on ceremony as we used to, and I am glad. But there is a thin line between informality and Christian courtesy. There is such a thing as good taste and the watchful observance of the rights of others. Everybody you

meet hurts somewhere. You must be careful not to make him hurt any more through your carelessness. If you can, find where the person is hurting and apply a little love and compassion.

Paul says, "See then that ye walk circumspectly, not as fools, but as wise, redeeming the time, because the days are evil" (Ephesians 5:15, 16).

This principle of knowing the difference between informality and carelessness applies in interpersonal relationships. Brashness can turn a person off; friendliness can win him.

We need to guard against carelessness in dress—we ought to look well for Christ's sake; carelessness in speech—spice in the vocabulary often turns out to be minced oaths; carelessness in business relationships—we need to do precisely what we promised. Especially must we be watchful of how we treat one another at home.

John G. Paton, the great missionary to the New Hebrides, tells in his autobiography of his early years in Scotland. The whole family lived in a cottage made up of a large kitchen workshop, a small closet-like room, and a bedroom that accommodated the entire family. Paton recalls that his father would do his work in the workshop and then, three times a day after meals, he would go into the closet between the two main rooms. The family knew that when that door was closed, the father was kneeling down praying for them. There were eleven children born of the union of James and Janet Paton, and at the judgment every one of them will stand at the mention of their parents' name and call them blessed.

That's what I'm talking about. It wasn't a formal household. You can't be very formal with eleven people in two rooms! But it was a God-fearing, God-honoring, prayer-filled home.

Don't criticize your wife or your husband in public, not even under the guise of joking. Don't be bombastic in your treatment of the waiter or waitress in a restaurant. Don't drive your automobile in high-handed disregard of the law.

Remember that as a Christian you are always on duty. There is never a time when you can say it doesn't matter.

The Lordship of Christ

There is no substitute for the lordship of Jesus Christ. Your whole lifestyle will be changed if you make him *Lord.* Anything less than his complete control leads only to hypocrisy.

The real reason, says Paul, behind the Calvary sacrifice was to make us believers totally Christ's own. Look at Romans 14:7-9: "For none of us liveth to himself, and no man dieth to himself. For whether we live, we live unto the Lord; and whether we die, we die unto the Lord: whether we live, therefore, or die, we are the Lord's. For to this end Christ both died, and rose, and revived, that he might be Lord both of the dead and living."

He must be Lord of the mind. 2 Corinthians 10:5: "Casting down imaginations, and every high thing that exalteth itself against the knowledge of God, and bringing into captivity every thought to the obedience of Christ."

He must be Lord of the body. Romans 12:1,2: "I beseech you therefore, brethren ... that ye present your bodies a living sacrifice, holy, acceptable unto God, which is your reasonable service. And be not conformed to this world: but be ye transformed (metamorphosed) by the renewing of your mind." The body always reflects the order of the mind.

He must be Lord of every activity. Colossians 3:17,23: "And whatsoever ye do in word or deed, do all in the name of the Lord Jesus . . . . And whatsoever ye do, do it heartily." (That's our word "psyched up"!)

At The King's College we recently lost a professor by drowning. He was caught in a sudden squall as he was sailing the Hudson River. At our memorial service, the president of the choir gave a word of tribute, along with many others. He said, "The thing I remember about Dr. Arlton is that he was completely dedicated to Jesus Christ *as Lord.* To him the Christian life was really very simple: either you obey the Lord or you don't."

To make him Lord means to turn over to him every

contested territory. It means to welcome him into the totality of your life. The amazing thing is that when you thus invite him, he *will* come in. "Behold, I stand at the door, and knock," He says. "If any man hear my voice, and open the door, I will come in to him, and will sup with him, and he with me" (Revelation 3:20). That is a great thought!

We have considered seven great thoughts. Add your own to the list. Ponder them well. Let the Holy Spirit use them, and the Word of God from which they are drawn, to change your life.

If these great thoughts become an intrinsic part of your lifestyle, the people you meet should see a new you. You'll be transparent.

13. Look —You're Transparent!

"Ah," my Latin friend would say to me with a twinkle in his eye, "I possess your numero!" Which is another way of saying, "I've got your number, I size you up well."

Ultimately the people we live with, the ones we work with, even those with whom we casually rub shoulders are going to know quite accurately the kind of person we are. The sad stubborn fact is that people can see right through us. We "cover our tracks" only lightly.

Billy Graham tells the story of a small boy (I suspect it might have been himself) who was warned by his father not to get into the family watermelon patch because, the father said, the melons were not yet ripe.

But one day when the father drove into town the boy could not resist the urge to show his superior knowledge of growing things. He found a melon exactly "right" for eating. Taking it to the back pasture he broke it open and buried his face in its cool heart. (It was *almost* sweet.)

The remains he hid in sandy soil beside the creek, covered carefully with leaves.

A few weeks later the father looked everywhere for a lost cow. His search took him to the back pasture. And there, of all things, were the first shoots of a watermelon patch! What happened next needs no explanation.

We might say that this story could apply to the fact that God sees hidden things in a person's life. He does. But people see them too.

I'm no advocate for wholesale exhibitionism, so to speak, in religious matters. There are some things that one may very well carry with him, unshared, to the grave. I don't think it helps people—either you or your hearers—to drag

out matters that ought to remain covered by the grace of
God. What I *am* saying is that our contacts with people show
us up to them. We are, as they see us, generous or selfish,
humble or proud, honest or hedging. Paul recognized this
transparency.

You Know Me

Paul (in 2 Timothy 3:10-15), addressing his "son" in the
gospel, enumerated some of the things he knew Timothy
could perceive in him.

"Thou hast fully known [me] . . . my doctrine [teaching]
. . . . manner of life . . . . purpose . . . . longsuffering . . . charity [Calvary love] . . . . patience . . . . persecutions, afflictions
. . . ."

What persecutions and afflictions?

They "came unto me at Antioch, at Iconium, at Lystra:
what persecutions I endured: but out of them all the Lord
delivered me." (And Paul added, *"All* that will live godly in
Christ Jesus shall suffer persecution"—remember that,
Timothy, not just you, not just me, but *all*.)

Then, Paul says, there will be others to encounter, "evil
men and seducers (imposters) shall wax worse and worse,
deceiving, and being deceived."

What is Timothy to do?

"Continue thou in the things which thou hast learned
and hast been assured of, knowing of whom thou hast
learned them. And that from a child thou hast known the
holy scriptures, which are able to make thee wise unto
salvation through faith which is in Christ Jesus."

Thus Paul spells out for Timothy—and for us—the blessed, God-given antidote for human nature faults on the one
hand and apostasy and rejection on the other.

And he says, in effect, "As you face these testing experiences, Timothy, people will see through you. They will
know whether you are genuine or not."

Your Doctrine Shows

"Thou hast fully known my doctrine." "Doctrine" is our

word teaching. You have to know what you believe before you can live it. And "know" here means you've gotten hold of truth independently, for yourself.

We have what we call the Second Generation Problem. Young people come to The King's College, or other schools, without a clear understanding of what they believe. To be sure, Mom and Dad are dear, dedicated Christians. They established a Christian home, and the son or daughter coasted along, presumably on the parents' religion. Then, by the young person's going away to school, the familiar props are removed. He suddenly sees that he must get hold of truth *for himself*—or he has nothing. Sometimes this realization is a great shock to him.

Paul says in effect, "Timothy, you 'know'; you have gotten hold of truth for yourself, independent of others. Good!"

What is the teaching (doctrine) in view here?

Teaching concerns the Word of God. The Christian position on the Bible is that it is inspired, that it was without error as God gave it in the original documents. The 66 books that comprise our Bible are substantially—I use that word carefully—the same as when our Lord gave them to those who wrote them in the first place.

The Bible agrees with itself. It is one unit. This could not possibly be true if it were not a miracle book, for it was written over hundreds of years, by many authors, in different cultures, at various times, and from many points of view. In spite of this diversity, "All scripture is God-breathed, and is profitable for doctrine (teaching)." See 2 Timothy 3:16. If you don't believe in an infallible Bible, of what good is it?

Six or eight years after I had used certain science textbooks in high school the idea struck me that I might sell these books to a second-hand dealer and get a few dollars for them.

The hoped-for buyer laughed at me. "These are out of date," he said, "we don't believe this stuff any more."

No, you wouldn't teach science from an outdated textbook, would you? Likewise if you don't believe the Bible is infallible, a book that is as up-to-date in its teaching about the cosmos as it is about spiritual matters—well, friend, what's the use of teaching at all?

At The King's College we believe in the infallible, inerrant, inspired Word of God, the Bible. Every scientist has the right to one presupposition; that's ours. Every time I have brought that up to a skeptical examiner who has come to look us over, he has had to agree: You have a right, academically, to your basic presuppositions as long as you keep consistent to them.

Teaching has to do with God's revealed purposes for this world. That takes in the sinfulness of man . . . . the holiness and love of God . . . . the redeeming work of the Lord Jesus Christ . . . . the blessed presence of the Holy Spirit.

Teaching relates to the character of the church. It is the Body of Christ—with Christ himself its living head. Though its members may be separated from one another by miles and denominational differences, they are one living organism.

Teaching relates to the desire of a gracious God for the evangelization of the world, leading to the second coming of the Lord Jesus Christ. He is "not willing that any should perish." Surely everybody in the world deserves the right to hear the gospel once before others hear it more than once.

Teaching relates to conduct. We are to live separate from the world system. "Know ye not," Paul says, "that your body is the temple of the Holy Ghost which is in you, which ye have of God, and ye are not your own? For ye are bought with a price: therefore glorify God in your body, and in your spirit, which are God's" (1 Corinthians 6:19,20).

There you have a quick over-view of some of the things that are important: the Word of God . . . . the Son of God . . . . the Gospel of God . . . . the Church of God . . . . the glory of God.

This, then is a wrap-up of Christian doctrine. It is something you and I need to *know.* Do you really know what you believe? Do you have a good working knowledge of the Word of God?

I would recommend to you a classic in its field, a book by the late Dr. R. A. Torrey entitled *What the Bible Teaches.* If you are near one of the Bible Institutes or Bible Colleges that teach the Word, where you could take courses, do that. Consider a Bible correspondence course. In any case and by any means, it is very important that you and I *know* what the Bible teaches—that is, doctrine. The person who bases his religion only on his feelings has an up-and-down experience, because feelings vary with the weather. Study the Bible, and your faith will stand firm, whatever happens.

I need no other confidence
  I have no other plea,
It is enough that Jesus died
  And that he died for me.

Know that. Your doctrine will be translated into daily living.

Your Manner of Life Shows

"Thou hast fully known . . . my manner of life." What you believe results in how you behave. For illustration, consider this hypothetical case.

Here's a man who has been caught breaking and entering—caught red-handed. He's brought to the police station and booked for attempted burglary. In due process his hearing is held. You think you know some mitigating circumstances and so you go to bat for him. As a result he's given parole. While he was in jail he was thoroughly repentant. But he's out now. You watch him, hopefully. To your surprise, in no time at all he's back at his old trade.

You say to him, "I thought you were through with all that."

He has a hundred alibis. The fact is, however, he still believes, down deep in his heart, that stealing is the easiest way for him to get his hands on some money—and so he breaks into people's houses and takes it. Not that he hasn't been told, by the judge and by you and a lot of other people, that what he did was wrong. The fact remains: *His belief has not changed, so his way of living is unaltered.*

Motivation is Important

Take another illustration. Here's this fellow who has been told that he has a stomach ulcer and that he therefore should stay away from highly spiced or fatty or acid or very fibrous foods. Well, he goes to dinner at Mrs. John Q. Citizen's house. She has some wonderful food, including watermelon pickles of which he is very fond. When passed his way, he takes a generous helping of pickles and of other things—two pieces of pie, the whole bit. He wakes up in the middle of the night with a terrible pain and calls the doctor.

"Now if this happens again," the medic tells him, "we're going to have to perform a gastric resection and take out maybe two-thirds of your stomach." (He might have added, "And all of your wallet.")

Something clicks in the man's mind and he thinks to himself, "Hey, what I did resulted in how I felt. I'd better watch that."

Thus he begins to believe what he didn't believe before. Now when he goes out to dinner and someone serves delicacies like watermelon pickles, he firmly passes them by and says, "No, thank you." Has he stopped liking watermelon pickles? No, he now *believes* what the doctor told him.

Belief Profoundly Affects Behavior

If you believe the will of God is good and acceptable and perfect, then you will be found doing the will of God. Paul did. He could say to Timothy, "You've fully known *my* manner of life."

Oh, yes. The way we live tells other people exactly what we believe. If you see a person who spends a lot on himself and little on his church, although he may sing loudly,

All to Jesus I surrender,
I surrender all,

you know he doesn't believe what he says.

Here's a young man who professes to be a dedicated

Christian, but he consistently runs with people of the world. He dates godless girls and his best friends are among those who have no time for God. He may say he's a Christian. He may get very "righteous" if you question him about it. But what he really believes is that the best crowd to go with is *his* crowd. His belief shows clearly in his manner of life.

I was talking years ago to a young person who had committed a felony—just gently probing to see how he felt about things.

He said, "Well, I know I'm in trouble. But I want you to know I'm a born-again believer and I'm as good a Christian as anybody else."

Bless his heart, maybe he was, and maybe he is, but at that point his lifestyle was giving the lie to his profession, wasn't it?

Value of Consistency

Parents sometimes come to me in great sadness. They say, "Where did we fail? We were faithful in the church. We took our children to Sunday School and saw to it that they were taught the Word of God. We tried to give them Christian upbringing in the home. Now they've turned against us and against the Lord. What went wrong?

I have to say first of all that it's not always a matter of parental failure when a child turns against the Lord. Christ himself told the story of the prodigal son, and the fact that the younger son took his journey into a far country and wasted his substance in riotous living certainly could not be ascribed to any misconduct on the part of that loving father.

But having said that, I must go on to point out that children particularly—although their observations are not well-organized—are amazingly acute and perceptive. When they see that religion is simply a veneer, when they see that it is something that can be put on on Sunday and chucked off for the rest of the week, they reject it. It's a frightening thought, isn't it? May it not be true that many a broken-

hearted parent could find the answer to his present distress
in the manner of life he has shown to his children over the
years?

Your Purpose Shows

"Thou hast fully known . . . my purpose." The way you live
grows out of the kind of purpose you have.

It's hard for me to tell somebody else what he or she
should be living for. We all know that the purpose of the
Christian is to glorify God, to be in his will, to do those
things that he planned for us from and to eternity.

Paul put the matter in a beautiful way in Philippians 1:20:

> According to my earnest expectations and
> my hope, that in nothing I shall be ashamed,
> but that with all boldness, as always, so now
> also Christ shall be *magnified* in my body,
> whether it be by life, or by death.

"Magnify" means to show up bigger and bigger. The
desire of every born-again believer should be that the Lord
Jesus Christ should be magnified—to entirely fill the frame of
our lives—so that people will see *him* when they observe you
and me.

Do you know how this is to be accomplished in your own
life?

First, your life must be *given* to him, so that he can live in
and through you. "I beseech you, therefore, brethren, by the
mercies of God, that ye present your bodies a living sacrifice
. . . unto God" (Romans 12:1).

Second, your loyalty and your standards must be *his*
rather than the world's. "Be not conformed to this world
[that means don't be jammed into the world's matrix or
mold] but be ye transformed by the renewing of your mind"
(Romans 12:2).

That word "transformed" is our word metamorphosis.
We know it as descriptive of what happens to a caterpillar
when it becomes a butterfly. Where once there were fifty legs,

now there are six. Fuzz has changed to wings and little whiskers have become beautifully colored microscopic scales on those wings. First there was the eating of leaves, now there is the tasting of nectar. A transformation has taken place!

Likewise the purpose of the Christian—to magnify the Lord Jesus—involves newness of life. Christlikeness is visible in a person in direct proportion to God's working of a miracle in that life.

Third, your desires must be wholly absorbed by his desires. Let his will be the determining factor in every decision you make. If you will do this, people will recognize his trademarks in your life (though they may never speak of this). When Christ's will is being done and Christ's work is being accomplished and Christ's power is being manifested, people will be able to say, as the Psalmist did, "This is the Lord's doing. It is marvelous in our eyes."

On some pieces of fine machinery and sporting equipment frequently you will find certain identification. For instance, if you buy an expensive shotgun and you look along the trigger guard you will find a tiny mark which is the personal trademark of the man who constructed that piece of equipment. It shows that the piece was handmade, carefully made, and that the manufacturer's stamp is on it.

What we want is the mark of God upon us. That's what the Psalmist prayed, "Let the beauty of the Lord our God be *upon* us."

For what purpose? So that Jesus can show up larger and larger in all that we say and do.

It is imperative that you and I line up our lives with the purpose of God in Christ. There are a number of verses that refer to this relationship. For example, look at Ephesians 3:8-11:

> "Unto me," [Paul said] is this grace given . . .
> that I should preach . . . the unsearchable
> riches of Christ . . . to the intent that now

> unto principalities and powers ... might be
> known by the church the manifold wisdom
> of God, according to *the eternal purpose* which
> he purposed in Christ Jesus our Lord: in
> whom we have boldness and access with
> confidence by the faith of him.

Could you say that your reason for living lines up with God's will? There is a phrase that's currently used, "getting it all together." Romans 8:28 says something like that: "We know that all things work together for good to them that love God, to them who are the called according to his purpose."

When you are in the will of God—and you know it— whatever occurs is not just happenstance, not accidental, not even coincidental. What takes place in your life and mine when we're in line with the purpose of God? We are made a part of God's eternal plans. We are brought into agreement with his all-encompassing holy will! Staggering thought, isn't it? Life for us "gets together." It doesn't fall apart, nor do we fall apart in it. There is a cohesiveness in living one's life in Christ that is a continual delight.

Look back over your life as I look back over mine. Can you see how he moved you from one place to another, from one environment to another, from one kind of work to another, from one challenge to a greater one? Every experience was necessary and good for the one it joined, wasn't it? Praise God for that.

You Purpose —God Works

"Daniel purposed in his heart that he would not defile himself" with the rich food and wine that Nebuchadnezzar the conqueror ordered for a select group of his captives. When Daniel declared his position, immediately he had support from his peers, Hananiah, Mishael and Azariah. They were in the 10-day test together. As one man, they came out with flying colors.

What happens when you make God's will your will?

When you obey God you'll find other people standing

with you—perhaps not many, but some. Look for them. Thank God for them.

You may have to pay a price for obeying God. There's an element of risk. It might just as well have been that Daniel's head, and those of his companions, would be cut off for suggesting disobedience to the king's command. Hebrews 11 speaks of glorious deliverances "by faith." But it calls attention also to some who "were stoned ... were sawn asunder ... were slain with the sword ... destitute, afflicted, tormented (of whom the world was not worthy)."

It says, *"These all ...* obtained a good report through faith." Obeying God involves willingness to do what he says, whatever happens.

When you do God's will you're assured ultimate victory. When the 10-day test that Daniel and his friends requested was over, "their countenances appeared fairer and fatter in flesh than all the children which did eat the portion of the king's meat" (Daniel 1:15). The blessings of that purposing extended through three dynasties. Daniel continued even unto the first year of King Cyrus.

This whole matter of an overriding purpose begins in the *heart,* with a sincere desire to live a holy life. Let me remind you that the world is full of people who are quite willing to talk religion but who back off when it involves their lifestyle.

A Question of Wanting

Many years ago I talked with a lady in a prayer room where she was kneeling after an evening service at which I had given a gospel invitation.

She said, "My husband warned me that if I ever became a Christian he'd leave me. I can't stand that thought!"

Whereupon she got up off her knees, put on her mink stole, went out and turned the key in her new Cadillac and drove off—unsaved. I haven't seen her from that day to this.

Do you really *want* God's will? I think we have to be honest here. There have been many times in my life when I haven't wanted to do God's will; I wanted my own way.

Well, then, what do I do about such a condition? Do I just go ahead and disobey? Oh, no. I pray, and by faith I commit my will to God, bringing every thought, as Paul says, "into captivity to the obedience of Christ."

If you are a child of God you took the Lord Jesus as Savior *by faith*, didn't you? Now how do you deal with any given need in your life? You take *by faith* his lordship, his mastery of that area. You give your unwillingness to Jesus by faith, and you take by faith his control of your motives. *He* makes the difference, the change in attitude and desire.

A cousin of mine, a high school principal, told me about a boy in his school who was a chronic swearer. But somehow he got in touch with the Lord Jesus Christ and his life began to change.

One day he injured himself in going over the high hurdles on the track. My cousin heard this story afterwards from the coach.

The coach said, "I went over to him where he was sitting on the ground hugging that injured knee and murmuring something to himself. The most I could hear was the phrase, "Don't let me do it! Don't let me do it!"

I said, "George, who are you talking to?"

"You wouldn't understand." He went on repeating, "Don't let me do it."

"Who are you talking to?"

"To Jesus."

"Don't let you do what?"

"Don't let me dishonor you, Jesus, by cursing and swearing."

He had learned the secret: Motives and actions are the natural outgrowth of *desire*—desire for the will of God. We take his control by faith.

Your Faith Shows

"Thou hast fully known . . . my faith." Faith is an observable phenomenon.

A good many years ago Youth for Christ was planning a

huge open air rally to be held on Memorial Day in Chicago's
Soldiers Field. Weather, as you know, in the upper Midwest
can be a bit capricious. In terms of advertising, rentals,
guarantees, radio outlay, etc., we had a good deal at stake for
we attempted not only to saturate the greater Chicago area
but also to reach out as far as Fort Wayne and Milwaukee.

At one of the pre-planning sessions somebody cautioned, "Don't you think that because we have so much
invested here we ought to have insurance agairst rain damage, so that if there is a storm that day we'll be covered?"

One person in the group—not a minister but a businessman—came up with a quick answer. His faith was observable. He said, "We believe God led us to do this planning,
don't we? We are *sure* God led us up to this point, aren't
we?" There was general, if unenthusiastic, assent. "Well,
then," our friend went on, "that being the case, I think it
would be gross unbelief on our part not to *expect* God to give
us all this project requires—including good weather."

There was no more mention of rain insurance. Incidentally, that Memorial Day it rained everywhere around Chicago
for a distance of some fifty miles. But in Chicago the skies
were blue! Hallelujah!

Is your faith observable, or is it something you keep well
hidden? Some people mask their unbelief under the pious
supposition that faith is such a private thing that they can't
talk about it. I've noticed that people talk about matters that
they're delighted about and that are important to them. The
reason some people don't talk about faith is that they don't
have any! Paul said, "You have fully known . . . my faith."

Trusting —and Cooperating

Faith is the ability to risk the situation on God, while
doing everything that he tells you to do.

Take, for illustration, Christ's feeding of the five thousand, as recorded in John 6. Jesus asked the question,
"Whence shall we buy bread, that these [a great multitude]
may eat?"

Philip replied in effect, "Why, Master, we'd have to go into debt for a whole year in order to give everyone just an hors d'oeuvre—and you know how mad a hungry man can get if he is served only a small bit!"

Jesus pressed the question: "What *do* you have?"

Andrew replied that they had only a boy's lunch—five black pancakes and two sardines. Jesus directed that the people be seated in companies of 50's and 100's (Mark 6:39). He distributed the food to the disciples and they in turn gave to the multitude, and they gathered basketsful of fragments left over. Jesus performed a miracle—because he is *God.*

Those portions of bread and fish did not magically float from his hands to the hands of other people. There were human beings whom God utilized in the process of performing this miracle. He uses *people* to do his will.

If you're interested in God's working through you in faith, make up your mind concerning two great realities: God is big enough to do anything. (You can safely risk all on him.) And your obedience is a part of his working.

Remember the incident recorded in John 9 about the man born blind. The Lord Jesus put some hand-warmed clay on the man's eyelids and told him to wash it off in the pool of Siloam. Could our Lord Jesus have healed the man without "means"? Of course he could! He did on other occasions give sight to blind people using only his word of power.

But here he wanted this man to be involved in obedience so that he—and we—could know the relation of obedience to faith and to a glorious outcome. When the man obeyed, he came back—seeing.

What is God asking you to do? Believe him. Risk the situation on him. Obey him. And you, too, will "see."

Focus on a Person

Faith is focused not on the trial or the testing, not on the experience or the circumstances, not on the job itself; it is focused on a person, the Lord Jesus Christ. Once you learn this lesson you will never be on the anxious seat about things that "happen." That's the thrust of the old song:

Faith, mighty faith, the promise sees
  And looks to God alone;
Laughs at impossibilities
  And cries, "It shall be done!"

Try this the next time you are under pressure and tend to worry. Look up and say, "Dear Lord, I'm yours. I'm trusting you in this situation. Show me what you want me to do. Teach me what you want me to learn."

You will be surprised at two results. The peace of God will fill your heart. Instead of fretting you'll be resting. You will also experience the joy of letting God work through your life, as you let him.

There is a verse in Isaiah (26:3) that points up this truth: "Thou wilt keep him in perfect peace whose mind is stayed on thee, because he trusteth in thee." The mind stayed on God is never a closed mind. The Bible nowhere teaches evasion of reality. We are to face facts squarely and honestly. But we are to face them with confidence that God is in charge.

This focusing of our faith on the Lord Jesus Christ will issue in our praying—not in generalities merely, but for specific objects.

We often quote the verse, "All things are possible to him that believeth" (Mark 9:23). Those words were spoken in the midst of great travail and heartbreak on the part of a father whose son was ill. He had taken his boy first to the disciples, but they could do nothing for him.

Now he pleads with the Saviour, "If *thou canst* do anything, have mercy on us and help us."

The Lord Jesus turned the phrase right back to the father and said, "If *thou canst*"—that is, "If thou canst believe, all things are possible to him that believeth."

Here was a specific need. The father brought it to our Lord Jesus Christ. And when his own heart began to believe God, the miracle took place. It is very easy to blame our troubles on other people when they actually originate in ourselves. "Canst *thou* believe?"

Simon Peter had the glorious experience of walking on the water at Jesus' command. But on that stormy Sea of Galilee, the moment his eyes strayed from the Saviour, down he went! As soon as he saw the wind and the waves boisterous, he became afraid and started to sink. It is always that way. But if I focus on the Lord Jesus—the Victor, the one who is always expressing the perfect will of God to me and through me—I'm on my way to victory.

Pray for specifics: If you need the mortgage paid for, don't just say, "Lord, help us." Pray in faith that God will lift the mortgage.

Other People Involved

Focused faith will also involve *people*. Mark 2 tells of four men who brought a sick man, their buddy, to the Lord Jesus. When they got to the house where Jesus was, they found the crowd so great that they couldn't get in, so they went to a back stairway, climbed up on the flat roof, took off the covering tiles, and let the man down through the hole they had made. The record states, "When Jesus saw *their* faith, he said unto the sick of the palsy, 'Son, thy sins be forgiven thee' (Mark 2:5). A moment later he said, "Arise, take up thy pallet and walk." He forgave him and healed him, in that order—all in response, mind you, to the faith of four people who believed he could do it.

Have you exercised faith for some one recently—some one outside the circle of your own family and close acquaintances? Have you seen a person in real need, and then prayed in faith about that need, and received by faith an answer from the Lord?

Yes, faith is an observable phenomenon. It is the ability to risk any given situation to God, while doing what he tells you to do. It is focusing one's attention—*steadily, consistently—on the Person of the Lord Jesus Christ, unafraid of conditions that surround us.*

Your Long-suffering Shows

"Thou hast fully known ... my long-suffering." In effect,

Paul was adding to what Timothy already knew about him. Paul implied: "You have found out about me. You have my number. You know what I taught (my doctrine), you know the way I lived (manner of life), you know the purpose that drives me and keeps me in touch with the power of God. Now, Timothy, you know of my long-suffering, too."

In the Greek the word is *makrothumia* . . . large-heartedness.

Long-suffering is a quality of God himself. "The Lord is merciful and gracious [long-suffering], slow to anger and plenteous in mercy" (Psalm 103:8). "The long-suffering of God waited in the days of Noah..." (1 Peter 3:20). "The Lord is long-suffering to us-ward, not willing that any should perish" (2 Peter 3:9). We are not surprised that the Apostle Paul states in Galatians 5 that the "fruit of the Spirit" is manifested in "love, joy, peace... *long-suffering*."

When we talk of a big-hearted person we think of one who is generous, outgoing, compassionate—one who cares, and cares enough to *act*. All of these concepts are involved in Paul's use of the word. He points out that this largeness of heart (that only God can create in and for his child) will have far-reaching beneficial results.

Long-suffering affects me personally. The capacity of my heart for God, and my capacity for caring about other people, are directly related to the authority I give to the Word of God in my life. Here is the secret: "I will run in the way of thy commandments when [or then] thou shalt enlarge my heart" (Psalm 119:32).

Long-suffering and patience are so closely entwined that it is impossible to speak of one apart from the other. We have to admit quite frankly that all of us are normally, naturally, impatient. For the most part, your average human wants things to *move*. Isn't that true?

Help Needed!

Sometimes we tend to defend our impatient ways. I remember a soprano who, many years ago, threw a tantrum in my office. When she had time to think of how she had acted she came back, a little ashamed of herself.

"Well," she said, "I blow my top—but then I get over it."

I tried to explain to her—gently, I hope—that one can indeed express his or her violent feelings and recover from the experience, but other people who are a part of that experience may not. Scar tissue may be left on their hearts that often never heals.

We must realize that we can't help ourselves, beyond a certain point. Self-discipline is good and we ought to practice it. But we may very well take a lesson from the Psalmist (Psalm 39:1-5) who wrote:

> I said, I will take heed to my ways, that I sin not with my tongue . . . (But) while I was musing the fire burned: then spake I with my tongue, Lord, make me to know the measure of my days . . . how frail I am . . . Verily, every man at his best state is altogether vanity.

That's what the Psalmist said even after he made up his mind to exercise self-discipline in the matter of his wayward speech. Like him, I must have someone to apply the life-changing truth of the Word of God to my life. That someone is the blessed Holy Spirit.

In Romans 5:5 Paul states that the "love of God is shed abroad in our hearts *by the Holy Ghost* which is given unto us." Here is divine compulsion; the love of God drove him along. Face up to the fact: no one of us can become large-hearted, in the scriptural sense, by his own efforts, try as hard as we may.

Newness Needed

I must be ready to change. The secret is spelled out in 2 Corinthians 3:18 where the key word is "changed."

> We all, with open face beholding as in a glass the glory of the Lord, are *changed* into the same image from glory to glory, even as by the Spirit of the Lord.

What that verse is saying is that if you get into the Word of God and let it get into you, a change will take place—and it will be a change heavenward. You'll get to be more like the Lord Jesus Christ. The one who accomplishes this continuing transformation, Paul says, is the Holy Spirit.

I *need* to be changed.

Projecting Christlikeness

The person that I really am will show up under pressure. Give me enough stress, that is, make me either tired enough or upset enough or angry enough or discouraged enough to damage my religious facade, and I will revert to the person I really am. It is very easy to mistake our professional appearances, so to speak, for the real life within. But people around us are not fooled one bit!

They watch to see how we react when the washer fails or the clothesline snaps. They look at us closely when they know something breaks our heart. They want to know how Christian faith relates to a hospital experience . . . to an accident . . . to a son's or daughter's brush with the law.

Perhaps a corporate merger has squeezed you out of a job after you have worked for the company for say forty years. People want to know how you "take" that ultimatum. With a combination of bitterness and panic you may be saying to yourself, "I gave that firm the best years of my life. Now look at me. What am I going to do? Nobody wants a man my age."

Dear fellow believer, look to God to "change" you at this point, to give you divine calmness and assurance "that the world cannot give." Remember, your peers are keenly scrutinizing you to see if you have what it takes to come out victorious.

We ought to specialize in other people's needs rather than our own. Try this yourself sometime: Spend one whole day seeking to help other people in every way you can, forgetting yourself in the process. I can guarantee that at the end of the day you may be weary, but you will also be very, very happy. You will have learned a great deal about long-suffering.

Paul tells us that there is another important aspect of this subject.

Long-suffering has a strengthening effect.

God's goal for me is not that I should just grin and bear my troubles, but that I should be strengthened in order to experience these things with God's power and God's joy. That's a tremendous concept, isn't it?

Paul wrote to the church at Colossae (Colossians 1:9-11):

> (I) do not cease to pray for you, and to desire that ye might be filled with the knowledge of his (God's) will in all wisdom and spiritual understanding; That ye might walk worthy of the Lord unto all pleasing, being fruitful in every good work, and increasing in the knowledge of God; *strengthened* with all might, according to his glorious power, unto all patience and long-suffering with joyfulness.

When Paul says "strengthened," he uses the word *duname* which is related to the noun *dunamis* from which we get our English word dynamite.

"With all might"—that's the Greek word . . . . which means literally a bulldozer-kind of strength that nothing can withstand. Did you ever see one of those big earth-moving machines that can lift say thirty cubit yards of earth at a time and carry it along at fifteen to twenty miles an hour? They can actually chew up a mountain in less time than it takes to write a book about it.

What God wants to do is to so work in my life that his power will be shown, not in my thrashing around and throwing my weight here or there so to speak, but in keeping me from blowing up, or giving up, or caving in, or exploding, or whatever. The purpose of God in strengthening me is that I might be patient, and the purpose of God's power is that I might have long-suffering—with joyfulness.

Long-suffering is a divine leverage by which God works.

This whole matter of long-suffering turns out to be God's blessed leverage to move other people closer to Jesus. The next time you are under pressure, think of it this way: God will use your long-suffering, your large-heartedness—not simply to make you able to "take it," but also that by this very means someone else will be drawn closer to our blessed Lord. Great truth, isn't it?

This thought is borne out in 2 Corinthians 6:4-10, where some of the ways of implementing our religious beliefs are listed. Note that each one is preceded by the little word "by";

By pureness . . . A person whose life is not holy can't be much of a blessing to others.

By knowledge . . . A person who is deliberately ignorant of God's Word and conditions around him can't help others very much.

By long-suffering . . . The one whom God has made large-hearted is the one who has a ministry to his peers. It is not simply that I am to be a certain kind of person and have a certain kind of reaction to life. That's true, I *am* to be long-suffering—that large-heartedness, that willingness to take . . . and take . . . and take without giving in or blowing up—*in order to* bring others closer to the Saviour. (Read the whole passage.)

All right. I admit I have a ministry to others. What is the atmosphere in which this ministry must flourish? The first verses of 2 Corinthians 6 spell it out: "afflictions . . . necessities . . . distresses . . ." Do you have any of these?

Remember, our job is to *give* God *to people*—not to win arguments, not even to show ourselves as being good Christians, not merely to enjoy a sense of well-being and satisfaction, all of which may come. But they are by-products. Our main business is to *minister* to people, and we often do this best through our own deep hurts, when they are yielded to God.

Is this clear to you? Long-suffering comes through God's Word. It comes through his Holy Spirit. It comes through his touch upon your life. It comes—oh, yes, it does!—as a result of testings he sends.

Don't fight them. Glory in them. Let God use them—in your own life and in the lives of others.

Your Charity (Calvary Love) Shows

"Thou hast fully known my . . . charity (Calvary love). Paul had already mentioned to Timothy several things that Timothy was aware of: Paul's teaching, his manner of life, his purpose, his long-suffering. Now, in effect, he says, "Timothy, you know also the special kind of love I have for you and for others; it is the love of God; it cannot be counterfeited."

In the King James Version of the Bible (I Cor. 13:1), the word is charity—our word for love. And it is a special kind of love that is in view here.

In the Greek language three words are translated "love": *eros,* which is sexual love; *philadelphia,* which is brotherly love, and *agapé,* which is divine love, the kind expressed in John 3:16.

When you get to know a person you find out quite accurately what kind of love (if any) he has and shares. Does he have anything more than the human capacity to be nice to other people who are nice to him or to whom he belongs in some familiar relationship? That person knows little or nothing about agapé love.

Agapé love starts with God. That's where you begin, not with yourself. Look at the kind of love God has: He "commended his love toward us in that while we were yet sinners, Christ died for us." The proof and the depth of God's love is the death of Christ on Calvary for a world of unconverted sinners. He proved his love by coming down the stairways of the stars, being born of Mary's virgin womb, living a sinless life, dying a perfect and atoning death on Calvary's cross and then rising, to be our living Saviour.

You say, "I wish I had more love."

Well, come to Christ. When you do, the love of God is shed abroad in your heart by the Holy Ghost who is given unto us.

In the fifth chapter of Galatians (v. 22), where Paul is speaking of the fruit of the Spirit, he puts love first.

The fruit of the Spirit is *love*, joy, peace, long-suffering, gentleness, goodness, faith, meekness, self-control.

Someone has said that in this Galatians passage every subsequent word is the result of love in a special sense.

Love begets joy.

Joy is love rejoicing.

Peace is love resting.

Long-suffering is love opening its heart to people.

Gentleness is love refusing to be unkind.

Goodness is love seeking the righteousness of God.

Faith is love trusting the almightiness of God.

Meekness is love bowing low enough to realize from what it has been saved.

Temperance, or self-control, is love turning over the reins of life to God.

This is agapé love in action. We ought to pray that God will give us more of it.

You say, "But I don't *feel* loving toward so-and-so." Years ago I learned from Bill Bright of Campus Crusade the great truth that I may take *love* by faith—even for that person whom I naturally resent—in the same way that I take *salvation* by faith.

Agapé love is the identifying mark of the Christian. It is the quality that sets him apart from others, that gives him distinctiveness.

Years ago, when I was five, or six, or seven years old, I lived in Cleveland, Ohio, with my father and my sister, our mother having gone on to Glory when I was a baby. At that time my father was caretaker at the Spencerian Commercial School and we lived in an apartment in the basement of the school. After class hours I was free to roam the building.

I used to like to station myself in front of a big plate glass window that looked out on busy Euclid Avenue where I could watch the cars rush by. I soon learned the names of the cars I saw, and after a while you couldn't stump me. All the old makes are gone now (and the mention of them dates me!): The Stutz, the Templar, the Mercer, the Pierce Arrow. There used to be a Chandler Chummy that was a kind of two-door, four-passenger affair, and you got in the front and then climbed through the middle of the front seat to get into the back seat.

Because I was so young, people often were surprised at my knowledge of these names.

"Oh," I would say, "I just look for the things that are *different* about each one." A Rolls Royce has that special radiator ornament. Another car has a unique fender. And so on.

Of course, this skill in identifying cars is not restricted to a past generation. Fellows and girls make use of it today. The principle holds: It is the *difference* that characterizes.

Has it occurred to you that Jesus gave the one identifying mark by which you are to be known as belonging to him? It's not your strictness, and it's not your aloofness, and it's not your theology neatly lined up in rows on the shelf of your soul. All of these things may be important, and of course they are. But Jesus said that if you want the heathen— anybody—to know that you belong to him, "By this shall all men know that ye are my disciples if ye have love one for another"—real Calvary love. It is that kind of love that sent the Lord Jesus to die for you. "Having loved his own . . . he loved them unto the end," John 13:1 says.

Agapé love—you simply can't fake it, because the Holy Spirit is the only one who can produce it, and when he does people will sense immediately the warmth of the divine presence. They'll feel safe with you. They'll be glad that you're around. And most of all they'll know—oh, yes, they'll *know*—that you belong to Jesus.

Agapé love must be experienced personally. Paul says the love of Christ is something "which passeth knowledge" and yet it can be known—in fact it *must* be known by each of us who claims to be Christ's follower.

As part of his prayer for the Ephesians (3:19) the Apostle

asked that they might "know the love of Christ which pas-seth knowledge [and] . . . might be filled with all the fullness of God."

That word *know* refers, not to intellectual enlightenment, but to personal experience. The difference between these two kinds of knowing came to me sharply more than 25 years ago.

I have always loved cars . . . motorcycles . . . airplanes . . . anything mechanical. At this particular time in my life I was reading avidly the current aviation magazines. I knew about different kinds of aircraft, what they looked like, the unique characteristics, their potentials, at what speed they might even stall out, and so on.

More Than Book Learning

I was riding with a fellow member of Youth for Christ in his Beechcraft Bonanza over Cuba to Jamaica and some of the other islands where we had a string of meetings. Well, it was great and I enjoyed every minute of it. Finally, I got my courage up enough to say, "Paul, you're a flight instructor and this ship has dual controls. How about giving me some instruction and letting me fly?"

"All right," he said, "let's do that."

He began by telling me that the thing most beginners do wrong is that they over-control.(In all my reading of avia-tion magazines, this problem had never impressed me.)

"Put just your thumb and forefinger on the control wheel there," he said, "and move them ever so slightly until you get the feel of the airplane."

I began to realize that a very slight movement on the control wheel would cause a considerable reaction on the part of the aircraft as it was making its way through the sky.

The tremendous import of what was happening swept over me. I was not merely reading about flying. I was experi-encing—personally, vividly—the awesomeness, the thrill, the responsibility of moving this flying machine. And you know what happened? I began to break out in perspiration because of the intensity of the effort to follow my teacher's instructions to not over-control, to keep the aircraft straight and level, moving on its assigned course.

What is the point here? Agapé love is much more than a doctrine to be studied. It is a personal thing—warming, moving, challenging, life-changing.

You can never do enough homework to understand the love of God. The Queen of Sheba came to see Solomon. After she had viewed the glories of his kingdom she said something like this, "I thought I knew a lot about you before I came here. But I have to tell you the half wasn't told me."

And that's the way it is with God's love. You can read about it. You can study it. You can talk about it. You can even pray about it. But until the Holy Spirit floods your soul with God's love, you really won't know too much about it. But you *may* know, and I pray God that you will. One thing more:

Agapé love can grow. Speaking of this love, Paul uses the word "abound" in Philippians 1:9-11:

> That your love may *abound* yet more and
> more . . . [you] being filled with the fruits of
> righteousness, which are by Jesus Christ.

Those of you who have been happily married for any considerable length of time will confirm what I'm about to say: As you have shared these years, and life has been good to you, you have grown to understand each other. It has been a blessed and a growing process.

"Abound" means to spill over. Suppose you had a cup filled with clear water and you were walking, let us say, from the kitchen to the dining room when somebody accidentally jostled you. What would spill out? Nothing but pure water. Nothing else *could* spill out, under those circumstances.

If indeed, however, you had something else—let us say some brown gravy in that cup, and you were jostled, then what would happen? The brown gravy would spill over and stain your clothing and the rug and all the rest.

Now I am not comparing the love of God to either pure water or brown gravy, don't mistake me. But I am saying that what is filling your life is what is going to overflow when you're bumped by the testing of life. Dear friend, you *can* have a life full of God's love—agapé love, that is, Calvary love—John 3:16 love—by trusting Jesus. It can fill every nook and cranny of your life—and overflow.

Your Patience Shows

"Thou hast fully known my . . . patience." The Greek word for patience is *hupomone* which means, literally, stay down, stay under. It's a picture word and its truth is hard for us to learn. We tend to want to be anywhere except "under." We jump up to assert ourselves. We blow off.

The mark of the amateur, the sign of the inexperienced, the characteristic of the immature person is that he feels he must *say* something. Simon Peter was that kind of person before Pentecost—always vocal. We read, "Simon answered and said . . ." Nobody had asked him, but he answered anyway! Many of us are like him.

Beware of the almost irresistible temptation to make a speech on something. It is better, the wise man said, to close one's mouth and be thought a fool than to open one's mouth and remove all doubt.

Most of my mistakes have been made in a hurry. Most of my embarrassments have come when I have jumped into a situation without knowing what it was all about.

One day a student delegation came into my office. I thought they wanted to discuss something about which I was already uptight. So before they spoke, I launched into my speech. When I paused for breath, the chairman of the delegation said rather mildiy, "Dr. Cook, that wasn't what we came to talk to you about." Was I embarrassed! I had lost patience, the ability to stay down.

Now that does not mean evasion or sidestepping. Someone is sure to say, "Well, Brother Cook, don't you believe in compromise?"

No, I don't. I believe your testimony—your stand for Christ—should always be clear and unwavering. But firm conviction need not involve your barging into a situation on which you are not thoroughly informed. Learn the score. Stay under.

Patience is a by-product, actually. We could cite any number of verses that would prove this point, but this one is familiar to all of us. Romans 5:3 "...We glory in tribulations also: knowing that tribulation worketh patience, and patience, experience; and experience, hope...."

This verse says that the troubles—and the pressures that they bring—all produce patience. Patience is the direct result of your having gone through certain hard experiences in which you found that God is *real.* Having learned this, you now are willing to wait on him the next time around. Patience is a product of tribulation. It also is a component part of growth. "Bring forth fruit with patience," we read in Luke 8:15.

My patience affects other people's lives. I think many of my mistakes have been made because I wasn't willing to wait for God to work in *other people's* lives. It's a dreadful mistake when we attempt to do something before God is ready.

Many years ago I found myself in the midst of a serious personality tangle—a situation that certainly needed to be righted. In my eagerness to have the trouble cleared up, I went to the people involved—and I came away scarred and broken. Why? Because that wasn't God's time. Later he himself worked things out beautifully. The air was cleared. God was glorified. *He* did it.

You don't have to insist on having your own way in lots of things in life. Have you learned that? Think back to the last time you had a quarrel with somebody, at home or work or school, with parents, children, husband or wife, brother or sister, whomever it was. Tell me this: How much of what was said or implied was eternally worthwhile? How much of it will be worth remembering a million years from now? (You'll still have your memory in heaven, you know.)

"Oh, well," you say with a little embarrassment, "it wasn't all that important, but it *seemed* important at the time."

Sure. I know. But patience will give you the long view. Paul says in 2 Corinthians 4:18:

> . . . look not at the things which are seen . . .
> for the things which are seen are temporal;
> but the things which are not seen are eternal.

It all depends on your point of view, doesn't it? And that attitude on your part profoundly influences those whose lives you touch.

Patience is a means of ministering. To "minister" is to impart, to share. Paul says (2 Corinthians 6:4) that we are to be found ". . . approving ourselves as the ministers *of God*, in much patience." The way we "minister God" is by being patient under circumstances that would cause others to give up or blow up.

The Apostle goes on to say what kind of patience is in view here:

"Patience in afflictions." . . . That means the troubles (different for each of us), that are a part of our daily existence.

"Patience . . . in necessities." These are the needs for which there is no foreseeable supply. What do you do when there is too much month left at the end of the money? That's the time to be patient with God because his timing is always right. And his supply is exactly what it ought to be.

"Patience . . . in distresses. . . ." That means the result you feel in your body, your mind, your emotions when you are going through trouble. I don't think it is unchristian to feel distress. Some say that if you are a good enough Christian you will never get upset by the things in life. But each of us is different from others in this respect and we react predictably according to the way we are built. Under pressure, some get ulcers, others high blood pressure, others headaches or any one of a number of other ailments.

The point is, you don't have to be a *victim* of your distresses. You can give your body and the way you are built to Jesus and let him manage the whole package that is *you*. It is possible for you to walk with God and exhibit patience even in the midst of the inevitable physical and mental strain that trouble brings upon you. As you do this, you will become a victor, not a victim. Hallelujah for that!

Patience . . . in opposition. Paul says they came unto him "at Antioch, at Iconium, at Lystra; which persecutions I endured: but out of them all the Lord delivered me."

Look at some of the kind of opposition Paul faced and out of which he says God delivered him. The account is in Acts 13:45-14:20.

There was opposition to success:

> When the Jews saw the multitudes [the whole city coming to hear God's Word], they were filled with envy, and spake against those things which were spoken by Paul, contradicting and blaspheming.

How did the Lord's servants react?

> Then Paul and Barnabas waxed bold, and said, It was necessary that the word of God should first have been spoken to you: but seeing ye put it from you . . . lo, we turn to the Gentiles . . . When the Gentiles heard this, they were glad, and glorified the word of the Lord as many . . . believed.

There was opposition from "chief" people:

> The Jews stirred up the devout and honorable women, and the chief men of the city, and raised persecution against Paul and Barnabas, and expelled them out of their coasts.

There was opposition from suspicion-venders:

> In Iconium ... the unbelieving Jews stirred
> up the Gentiles, and made their minds evil
> affected against the brethren.

There was opposition marked by great extremes.

> In Lystra, where the man crippled from birth
> was healed so that "he leaped and walked,"
> the crowd hailed Barnabas as Jupiter and
> Paul as Mercurius. When the apostles heard
> this, they rent their clothes and ran in among
> the people crying, "We also are men of like
> passions with you, and preach unto you that
> ye should turn from these vanities unto the
> living God."

The fickleness of humankind brought a violent change in attitude.

> There came certain Jews from Antioch and
> Iconium who persuaded the people [the
> same people who were ready to worship the
> apostles the day before], and having stoned
> Paul, drew him out of the city, supposing he
> had been dead. Howbeit, as the disciples
> stood round about him, he rose up and came
> into the city; and the next day he departed
> with Barnabas to Derbe.

There you have it—patience in the midst of opposition of all kinds ... people talking ... conspiring against you ... following you from place to place ... stirring up trouble ... even at times premeditating physical injury to you.

There is a thin line between persecutions and afflictions—and their relation to opposition.

Persecution is the trouble that is caused by the people who are opposing you religiously.

Affliction is the pain and the inconvenience that come ofttimes as the *result* of persecution. I would not be surprised if Paul walked with a limp for many a day after he was stoned.

Persecutions and afflictions—because Paul had them both he has a heartening word for each of us who suffers testings in any measure similar to his.

Your Response to Trouble Shows
"I endured . . . out of them all [persecutions and afflictions] the Lord delivered me."

The key word that describes Paul's attitude toward all his testings is "endured." He says in effect, "I stuck it out; I went through all of them." How does one do that?

Let me give you an illustration. Suppose it is Monday morning—and you are a minister. Yesterday you preached your heart out more than once. You didn't see too much response to the Word. Now you wake up tired and blue. (Unless you have been a pastor you don't know how discouraged you can get.)

This is the time for you to do three things: scan the long panorama of God's goodness to you, realize that he is doing something great in your own life, and rejoice over the immensity of the plan he will unfold.

Look back and see what the Lord has done for you in the months that you have served that particular pastorate. I used to get a great deal of encouragement from periodically reviewing just how many prayers I had seen God answer for me since I began in that church.

"Consider what great things the Lord *hath* done"—note the past tense.

"There hath not failed one word of all his good promise," Solomon declared, in I Kings 8:56.

God keeps His word—remember that. People may be faithless from time to time but God is ever faithful. Look back and see!

Then realize God is doing something great in *you*.

I can see different stages of development in my own life in the ministry that were directly traceable to the kinds of experiences I had at the time. All along, the Lord was doing something *in me.*

Again, catch a glimpse of the greatness of God's plan that includes you.

Dr. V. Raymond Edman, who for many years was President of Wheaton College and my dear friend, used to say, "It's always too soon to quit—always."

There are times, of course, when change is called for, when it is definitely in the will of God for the individual. At such times his child may clearly hear his words, "Behold, I will do a new thing." He may very well move you from Timbuktu to Kalamazoo, or some other distance—but that does not mean you have to quit an assignment because it is hard or because you yearn for greener pastures. Let's all remember that God isn't through with us yet; he is working out a perfect master plan. There is a great deal more that is waiting to be accomplished. Will you remember that the next time you are tempted to quit? Paul endured. You and I can well learn from such an attitude.

"Endure" to Be "Delivered"

The other key word that is as important as "endured" is in the phrase "the Lord *delivered* me." When you get that combination you are invulnerable (that means you can't be shaken up), and you are invincible (you can never be conquered). This combination in your attitude toward trouble—especially the kind that comes from people's opposing your faith in Christ—makes you secure and immovable.

If you want to go God's way, you must *expect* opposition. "All that will live godly in Christ Jesus shall suffer persecution." It's part of the mix.

Jesus said plainly (in Mark 10:29):

> There is no man that hath left house, or
> brethren, or sisters, or father, or mother, or
> wife, or children, or lands, for my sake, and
> the gospel's, but he shall receive an hundred-
> fold now in this time, houses and brethren,

and sisters, and mothers, and children, and lands, *with persecutions;* and in the world to come eternal life.

Again he said:

If the world hate you, ye know that it hated me before it hated you. If ye were of the world, the world would love his own: but because ye are not of the world, but I have chosen you out of the world, therefore the world hateth you (John 15:18, 19).

The antipathy of the unsaved person toward Jesus is built in. My friend David Morken, who has served on several mission fields, used to say, "The unsaved heart cannot rest until it is organized in opposition to God—that is its goal." That's a very cogent statement isn't it?

We speak of something "given" as that which is essentially and inevitably a part of a situation. In a triangle, for example, it is inevitable that it has three sides. Likewise, if you belong to Jesus, one of the "givens" is opposition. Expect it. You can't avoid it, but you can glory in it.

What happened? Paul says, "The Lord delivered me"— not out of a few persecutions, not out of a few afflictions— but "out of them *all*."

He will do that for us, too. It is our part to "endure" (by his own gracious enabling of us); it is his part to "deliver"— fully, gloriously. He has not brought you this far, my dear Christian friend, only to forsake you. He does not propose to dump you now. He is going to see you through. You can depend upon your blessed Lord Jesus who said, "Lo, I am with you *all the way* even unto the end of the age."

Inevitable Transparency

Just as Timothy "knew"—and quite accurately—the characteristics of his honored mentor, the Apostle Paul, so our peers can see through each of us. What they observe is the true picture; we can fake nothing.

Every day of our lives we show what we actually believe. We do it by the way we live, by the goals we set, by the tenderness and patience (or lack of them) that we show, by the depth of Calvary love we both enjoy and share. People see through us—oh, yes, they do!

Are we startled by this inescapable truth? We ought to be.

What shall we do, then? Shall we try harder to do better? We all know from experience that human efforts always fall short of divine completeness.

Rather, let us daily be found "looking [off] unto Jesus, the author and *finisher* of our faith" for the transformation in our lives that he waits to accomplish . . . day by day . . . week by week . . . as we trust in him.

Amy Carmichael, in her book called *Gold Cord*, tells of watching a goldsmith refine gold after the ancient manner of the East. In the red glow of the charcoal fire lay a common curved roof tile. This was the crucible. In it he placed certain "medicines" calculated to help purify the molten gold. "How do you know when the gold is purified?" asked Miss Carmichael. That beautiful Indian smile lit up the man's face as he replied, "When I can see my face in the molten gold in the crucible, then it is pure!"

Yes, people do see through us—an inescapable fact. But in answer to prayer and by divine grace, what they see can be a reflection of his beauty, his holiness, and his peace!

Now let's turn to your conversation. Your walk with the King should be reflected in that also. But some Christians talk in ways that make people tune them out. Why? How can you talk about Christ in such a way that people will listen to you—eagerly?

14. Does Anybody Listen to You?

When you speak, does anybody really listen? Does your message get through to the hearer in the way you meant it to do? The answers, and many others, involve the important subject of communications.

We are inclined to regard any in-depth study of this theme as being intensely modern. But Job, the oldest book of the Bible, has something pertinent to say about it. The patriarch asks some penetrating questions related to what God has done and will do for and through the believer. Note the verbs: "helped," "saved," "counselled." The final point in this series (Job 26:1-4) is "plentifully declared," which I take to refer to the whole idea of meaning, of communication in its fullest sense.

Communication begins deep inside your life. It doesn't start with what you say. It doesn't even begin with what you do. It begins in what you *are.* People know what you are without your saying very much. Ladies, were you ever introduced to some man and you immediately thought, "I don't like him"? You had known him less than thirty seconds, but something about him said, "Watch out." Later you found out he was the office wolf. But your woman's intuition (ignition, I call it) came up with quick evaluation and warning.

Can you tell when somebody likes you? Yes, you can. Can you know when you are being merely tolerated? Of course you can. So it is the inner person to whom you have to give careful attention. Remember, we often communicate without saying a word. The lectures that we give people are seldom retained, but the lessons they learn through obervation—by absorption, osmosis, so to speak—are carried

144

through life. If you occasionally tell a "white lie" to get out of an embarrassing situation, you are teaching your children that truth isn't nearly as important as saving one's own hide. It's the inner person to whom you have to give careful attention.

A physician friend of mine told me he could usually recognize the personality profile of his patients simply by observing them as they came into his office. He described one lady to me and said, "I knew she was full of resentment the minute I laid eyes on her, without ever having heard about her or examining her, because everything about her was sharp-edged. She had a long quill sticking out of her hat and every other ornamentation she wore was sharp-point-ed. Even her posture indicated resentfulness."

Well now, I suppose it would be a mistake to say that everybody who wears a feather in his or her hat is filled with resentment. But taken together, all of these indications told this man of medicine and of science something about the individual. Unwittingly, she was communicating something about herself.

Sure enough, when she told the doctor her problems, it had two main symptoms. She had a sore aching neck and she had pains across her chest that she attributed to heart trouble.

The doctor put her through all the pertinent tests and conscientiously analyzed them. Her heart was fine—beating strongly and regularly—and there seemed to be no real physical problem with her neck. He began to ask her some questions and found out that she was terribly jealous of her husband's mother and that these attacks would come on generally coinciding with visits from her mother-in-law. The last attack had been triggered by the fact that the dear old lady had fallen ill and had been taken to the hospital and the husband had taken money that she, the wife, had been counting on for something for the house and he bought flowers for his mother instead.

I don't know whether she ever did face her resentment

and got rid of it. The point I'm making is that we communicate our inner attitudes by the way we look and the way we talk and the way we act.

The wise man (Solomon) said it years ago: "Keep (guard) thy heart with all diligence" (Proverbs 4:23). Why? "For out of it are the issues"—the breaks, we'd call them—"of life." People say, "The breaks went against me." But we create our own "breaks." They are directly related to the lordship of Christ in the life. "No *good* thing will he withhold . . . ." And when your inner life is right with God, when you confess to him your daily need and are prayed up to date, the very presence of the Lord is communicated through you to other people.

Simon Peter and John, on their way to the three o'clock prayer meeting, were accosted by a beggar. You remember Peter's classic assertion: "Silver and gold have I none; but such as I have give I thee: In the name of Jesus Christ of Nazareth rise up and walk" (Acts 3:6).

What happened? Peter "took him by the right hand, and lifted him up: and immediately his feet and ankle bones received strength. And he leaping up stood, and walked, and entered with them into the temple, walking, and leaping, and praising God."

You communicate what you *are* as a result of God's grace in your life. And you communicate what you thus *have*, to others.

How do we communicate positively?

Concentrate

First, fill your mind with the Word of God. This is the only way to modify character and change conduct.

To do this you must *will* to fix attention on the Scriptures. Oh, you may have many fleeting thoughts around the edge of consciousness—I know that. But you can really concentrate on only one thing at a time. If you will thus devote yourself to the Word of God, and put it back into the unconscious mind so that it will come out of your "computer" when it is needed, you will find that two things happen: One, the intense effort that you have made to direct your mental powers toward the Word of God will leave little room for lesser things. And two, having put the Word of God into the computer portion of your mind, it will be *the Word* that will pop out when you are under pressure. The Psalmist makes this point clear. He says, "I thought on my ways"—that's *concentration* and it can come only as the Word of God is applied. "And turned my feet unto thy testimonies"—that's conduct. (See Psalm 119:59).

Do you know how to do this? Obviously you're going to read your Bible. But more than that is indicated. Meditate upon it. Choose key verses to memorize. Learn whole portions. Think about them during the day. Share them with others.

Remember how, when you were kids in school, you used to put a Lifesaver or something like it in your mouth when the teacher wasn't looking. You couldn't be seen chewing it, so you would slip it alongside your molars and hide it in the side of your cheek. Then once in a while when you thought it was safe you'd slip it out with your tongue and savor that good minty taste, and then you'd slip it back again. Remember that?

There are moments when you can slip a portion of God's Word into the tender area of your consciousness, so to speak, and you can meditate on it. You can enjoy it even for so much as thirty seconds. And then you have to get back into routines again. But for that brief period you were savoring, you were tasting, you were meditating on the Word of God. Form the habit. You'll be surprised how much it enriches your life. Later, you will find that you are speaking not necessarily in biblical terms but on the basis of the truth from God's Word which has taken hold of *your* mind and heart—and people will *listen*. You will be communicating God's thoughts. If you want other people to wonder what has happened to you and why you have improved so much, try soaking up large portions of the Word of God. Then your instinctive reactions to pressure situations will glorify God and bless others.

Depend

Second, learn to depend on the Holy Spirit. Our Lord Jesus said to his disciples on one occasion, "It is not ye that speak, but the Holy Ghost" (Mark 13:11). The Holy Spirit possesses personal characteristics: seeing, speaking, directing, etc. Note the great number of such declarations as these: "Peter, full of the Holy Ghost, said ..." "Saul, full of the Holy Ghost, said . . ." These verses tell us that the Holy Spirit will speak through a person effectively under certain circumstances. What are those circumstances?

You must know that you are God's child. The Spirit of God will not speak through you or use you unless you belong to the Lord Jesus Christ. If you have never settled that matter, you need to make this your first priority. No matter how religious you may be, you need to invite Jesus Christ into your heart and life to be your Lord and Saviour. Settle that. That's the beginning.

Next, be sure there is nothing in your heart that is still waging war against the will of God. It is difficult for God to use the person who is fighting him. The ancient prophet asked the rhetorical question, "Can two walk together except they be agreed?" (Amos 3:3). Two people can't walk together, if they go in opposite ways. Neither can your mind follow two sets of ideals successfully at the same time.

Years ago I asked a medical doctor—a man in charge of a large state hospital—"Doctor, is there any one reason why many of your patients are here?"

He replied, "Yes. Many of my patients are here because they tried to be true to two sets of ideals at one time." And he added, "Doesn't your Bible say something about no man being able to serve two masters?"

"Yes, sir," I said, "it does."

"Well, Preacher," he concluded, "you'd do us medical men a favor if you'd preach oftener on that." And he turned and walked away.

It is difficult for God to use a person who is not wholly yielded to him. If there are some unsurrendered pockets of resistance that need to be cleared out, well then, deal with them. Let the Lord shine the light of his Word upon you. Let him give you the power of his redemption and the cleansing and enabling presence of the Holy Spirit focused upon these very areas of your life.

If you are God's child, and you know you are yielded to him the best you know how—not perfect, but yielded and wanting God's will—if you know *that*, then you can depend upon the blessed Lord to guide you.

Focus

Third, learn to focus on the other person instead of yourself. This principle can be illustrated in many different ways. For example, if you were raised on a farm before the days of the sophisticated equipment that we have now, you know about plowing a field the hard way. What did you do to achieve a straight furrow? Did you keep looking behind to see if it was straight? No. You fixed your attention on a tree or a fence post or a hill or some other distant point and as you proceded toward it, the row was straight. We are to be "looking (always) unto Jesus, the author and finisher of our faith."

Now when you communicate with people, the same principle applies. Don't focus on yourself. Focus on the other person. How does he feel about things? What are his goals and dreams? What are his disappointments and heartaches? Where—if you can find out—is he hurting and would appreciate a word of comfort?

Years ago I read a series of little books on management. One of them said that the essence of negotiation is to ask these questions: First, what does the other fellow want? Second, what do I want? Third, how can we get together? That's oversimplification, but it is a workable formula.

God does something for you when your first concern is the other person. As an illustration, when you point that twelve gauge shotgun at something and pull the trigger, the charge of buckshot is projected out the business end of the barrel, but you feel a mighty kick against your shoulder. Similarly, God's power reaches you as well as the one you communicate with.

Dawson Trotman, founder of the Navigators, used to write on the palm of his hand with india ink the particular object of his attention that day—the person, the Scripture verse, or whatever. On one occasion I saw the letters "O.W." on his hand.

I said, "Daws, I don't know any of your workers who has those initials."

He laughed and said, "They don't stand for a person. They stand for "Other Works." and he quoted this verse: "Look not every man on his own things, but every man also on the things of others" (Philippians 2:4).

"Today," he said, "we are praying for other people in the Lord's work. As a matter of fact, we just got through praying for you as you came in." Isn't that beautiful?

I remember complaining to somebody years ago about a certain job situation, spelling out my troubles. The other person stood there listening and when I had finished he said, "You know, it's wonderful that you understand about me." All the while I was talking about me he was thinking about himself.

The other person is the center of his world. You may just as well realize it and count on it. So focus on his need—and he will listen to you. Consider another idea.

Language

Fourth, make sure that you and the other person are talking about the same thing. It is amazing how people can converse with each other with entirely different meanings to the words they use in common.

Learn to pin down generalities. Parents, of course, are familiar with what I am going to tell you. Your teenager comes home and says "May I do this or that?" and you say, "No, I don't think you should."

Your child replies, "Oh, Mom, you don't understand. Everybody's doing it."

Well, now, who is "everybody"? It turns out that Josie down the block is "everybody," and knowing that puts an entirely different cast on the whole situation. Define your terms. You hear: "It's only a little way." How far is a little way? "It will be only a little after midnight." How long after midnight? "There will be just a gang of the kids." Who are the kids, and how many are in the gang? If that sounds like cross-examination, it doesn't have to be. Just establish in your own mind and in the minds of your loved ones that you want to know what the facts are.

The mark of an educated person is that he quantifies and qualifies his statements. How much, how far, at what cost, and so on. Somebody said to me the other day. "I'm about to give up the whole thing." What did he mean? His marriage? His job? His house? I had to ask him. It turned out that "the whole thing" he was talking about was one small segment of his life. When he thought about it he decided he'd better not let that go either.

Learn to define your terms to yourself. You may think this is pretty dull, but do remember that it's terribly important. Be exact in your terminology, not pedantic, not pedestrian, not so terribly detailed that later, when you speak, you put everybody to sleep. I'm simply saying that you need to think clearly about what you mean before you say it. It will save you many a painful situation afterwards.

We don't go around preaching to people in the ordinary course of daily affairs. But our main business in life is to share Christ with them. Well, then, if you really want to communicate with people, isn't it worth the trouble and time it takes to think out what you mean before you speak?

I would be the first to admit that oftentimes I speak quickly and without thinking. They say my mother had a sharp although gentle Irish tongue and I think I inherited some of the sharpness at least. So I admit that I need to apply what I'm telling to you. But we're all in this together, because we're human beings. And if we want to communicate Christ to people, let's learn to be very sure of what we believe and let's say it in terms of the other person's interests and needs.

Organization

Fifth, in terms of work to be done, be sure you and your listener are talking about the same things.

There are six questions to be asked, and the answers found, if you want to organize anything.

First, what is to be done? (Many people get into arguments about the *how* before they have settled the *what*.)

Second: Who is to do it?

Third: How is it to be done?

Fourth: By what time is it to be finished? (Always set a deadline.)

Fifth: How much will it cost?

Sixth (a supplemental evaluative question): How well was it done? Always have a post mortem so you can learn from your mistakes.

On this matter of improved evaluation you can do three things to help yourself. Just before you close your day, go over the things you did and said that day and ask: How can I do better next time? Then plan, in order of priority, the activities of tomorrow. (Better to plan them at night than later, when the day begins. The list will change, of course, but you will be surprised at how much you accomplish.) Finally, speak to your blessed Lord and let him speak to you so that the last word in your consciousness is the Word of God. Drift off to sleep with a passage of Scripture in your mind and you'll wake up with a blessed awareness of God in your life.

Listening

Sixth, play back to your friend what he has said to you. The formula is simple. A tells B; B tells A what he understands; then A tells B he understands B understands! If you really want to communicate, play back in your own words what people want you to grasp, and vice versa. You'll often hear, "No, that's not what I meant at all!" It is like the video tape that is backed up and replayed on a close call at second base. This matter of playback takes a little time, but do be patient with people because, quite frankly, you expect them to be patient with you, don't you? Apply the Golden Rule: listen to others as you hope they will listen to you.

Many people don't really listen. They just wait for you to pause for breath so they can jump into the conversation. Someone has given a classic definition of a bore: He is somebody who insists on talking about himself when I can't wait to talk about myself.

Incidentally, you pay your listener a subtle compliment when you play back his thoughts to him. That person begins to feel safe with you because he knows you listen with great respect and interest—enough to put forth the effort of re-phrasing what he had said.

What do you do in the case of a wild idea that seemingly has no value to you whatsoever? Do you say, "That idea's absolutely way out in left field and doesn't make any sense"? If you do, you lose your audience immediately. Dr. Clyde Narramore gives a suggestion at this point.

You turn to your listener and say, "Well, you certainly have an idea there!" You haven't said whether it is a good idea or not, but you have acknowledged the intelligence of the listener. You could then go on to say, "I wonder if we could talk about it together"—and in the course of the ensuing conversation you might be able to show certain difficulties that would render the plan not feasible.

Whenever you are going to point out a weakness, say "we." When you acknowledge people and their worth, say "you." When you criticize say "we."

So far as your witness for Christ is concerned, you need to specialize on a few things that you can communicate well. I once saw a graphic demonstration of how little of what people hear is retained by them. Let us suppose you say ten different things to a person. How many of them does he remember? Experiments have shown that that person recalls no more than three. Then when that person, who remembers only three things, tells those three to somebody else, do you know how many get across? One, or none.

Learn to clearly spell out a few things: God's plan of salvation as *you* have received it, the walk of faith as *you* are enjoying it, the hope for the future as the Word of God outlines it. When you do this consistently, *people will listen to you*. Your own heart will be warmed and will be blessed. Try it!

This is not to say that everyone you talk to will agree with you. We live in a day of lowered standards and shifting values. But even if people don't agree with your Christian testimony, you know that there are some things you can always count on because God has told you that they are true.

15. Some Things You Can Always Count On

Suppose you are a navigator—whether of some ancient sailing vessel or of a sophisticated modern leviathan, it does not matter. You plot your course according to known unalterable guides. And you know that by following that set course you are absolutely certain of arriving at precise destinations.

The compass always points to the north. The stars in the heavens are spread out in a pattern of predictable exactness. You can count on the trustworthiness of this information.

But you are not piloting a ship. You are "just living."

Can you be sure that by giving strict attention to the eternal bearing points in the Word of God, you will arrive where you want to be?

You can!

Proof of this fact is in a exciting story recorded in Acts 3-4. Recall the scene:

Simon Peter and John had been accosted by a lame man and had healed him. This happening created no small stir, as you may well imagine! It accomplished two things: It gave Peter an opportunity to deliver a straightforward sermon as a result of which people were converted. It also resulted in Peter's and John's being thrown into jail.

The next morning these two were brought out, questioned, threatened and let go. (How could it be otherwise, with the healed man standing right there as living proof of God's miracle-working power?)

Now we come to the part of the story which shows clearly that there are predictable results that can be cited in the life of any believer who really wants to live for the Lord. Naturally, this brief portion does not enumerate *all* the results, but there are at least three here that we should look at.

155

And being let go (it says), they went to their own company, and reported all that the chief priests and elders had said unto them.

And when they (that is, the rest of the church) heard that, they lifted up their voice to God with one accord, and said, Lord, thou art God, which hast made heaven, and earth, and the sea, and all that in them is.

Then the inspired historian quotes these disciples of Jesus as saying:

Lord, behold their threatenings: and grant unto thy servants, that with all boldness they may speak thy word, by stretching forth thine hand to heal; and that signs and wonders may be done by the name of thy holy child Jesus.

Then what happened?

And when they had prayed, the place was shaken where they were assembled together; and they were all filled with the Holy Ghost, and they spake the word of God with boldness . . . .

And with great power gave the apostles witness of the resurrection of the Lord Jesus: and great grace was upon them all. (Acts 4:23-33).

Count on This —
You Pick Your Own Crowd

See what it says. "Being let go, they (the two representatives of Jesus Christ) went to their own company" (v. 23).

You choose your own crowd in life, and the people you like to associate with become an exact reflection of the person *you* are. (Oh, you say, what about those missionaries who can associate only with the lowest and least "spiritual" of men? The rule still holds, for those faithful ambassadors of

Christ are seeing their peers not as they *are*, but as they could be and will be, by the grace of God.)

It always works this way. If you are a playboy and live for conquests, you'll gravitate to that type of crowd. If you are a mocker, you'll join the scorners. If you're a practical joker, you'll search for the friendship of those like-minded.

On the other hand, if you want to find ones who love God, you'll find them. If in your heart there's a longing for prayer, divine guidance and the peace of God, you'll pick the people who have similar desires. If you really yearn for the salvation of the world, you'll probably be found with other people who, like you, believe that every one should hear, at least once, that Jesus Christ can save.

All of us have had experiences similar to one I recently had. As I was moving down a cafeteria line I noticed the lady behind the counter. She was efficient and friendly. But there was something else about her. She had a certain light in her face. I summoned my courage and said, "You're a Christian, aren't you?" But I knew the answer was "yes," before she said it.

Remember, you can't fake this relationship with the Lord. Your "own company" will tell on you every time. Peter found this out when he heard the biting reproof, "Thy speech betrayeth thee."

I beg of you, then, give some thought to the people in whom you invest time and friendship. Unmistakably, they will make something of *you*, and they will reveal a good deal *about* you, too.

Count on This —
Ultimate Victory Belongs to People Who Pray

Notice: "They lifted up their voice to God with one accord, and said, Lord, thou art God . . . ."

All of our lives most of us have heard about praying. Not all of us do a lot of it, but we've heard enough so that when someone talks about prayer we inwardly respond, "Oh, yes, I know about that. Let's get on to the next point."

But although it is almost a cliché, the fact remains that the victory any time, anywhere belongs to the people who *pray*. Prayer puts you in touch with Almighty God. And who is *he*? The verses tell us.

> . . .God of creation—"thou hast made heaven and earth";
> . . . God of inspiration—"who by the mouth of thy servant . . . said";
> . . .God of incarnation—"thy holy child Jesus";
> . . .God of eternal purposes—"thy counsel determined . . . to be done";
> . . .God of Calvary and the empty tomb— "witness the resurrection."

What more could you want? Yes, prayer puts you and God, in inverse order, in full command of any situation. And because God is *God*, there can be only victory ahead.

Prayer is important at The King's College. What the students learn here is not all that different from the curriculum that is offered at any one of some 2,000 other undergraduate institutions. We do require that courses in Bible be taken here. We do teach the liberal arts and natural sciences from the point of view of classic biblical Christianity.

But the difference between this school and the hundreds of others is found in a certain firm emphasis. We hold that whether a student chooses to be a scientist or a writer, a lawyer or a physician, an engineer or a housewife, a teacher or a missionary or any one of a number of other vocations, everything depends on the eternal dimensions of *God* in his life. And that is true for all of us. With him, we can do anything—absolutely anything—to which he is calling us. Without him in the inner throne room of our life, our most elaborate efforts will bring only scant, if any, success. Prayer helps us to "draw nigh."

Most of us put prayer last, rather than first in our list of priorities. We are like the dear lady whom Vance Havner tells about. She was greatly disturbed over many real and imagined troubles.

Finally, in a spirit of love (and some desperation) her family told her, "Grandma, we've done all we can for you. You'll just have to trust God now."

"Oh dear," she replied, despair on her face, "has it come to that?"

Vance Havner goes on to say, "It *always* comes to that, so we might as well *begin* with that." God's Word tells us to bring all our concerns to the Lord. When we do, the peace of God comes in—you can be sure of it.

My first introduction to "balance of power" praying came when I was just beginning to preach. Each Friday night, during the service at the Chicago Gospel Mission, we would be interrupted by the sound of some derelict being rolled—literally—down the stairs outside, by the owners of a bar upstairs.

The director of the Mission said, "We're going to pray those people out!" He invited me to stay with other friends for an all night prayer meeting.

A week passed, and we held another all night session of prayer. To our delight, during the following week, the people upstairs moved out, bag and baggage! The Mission director lost no time in renting the space for a sort of "halfway house" for men who had trusted Christ and wanted to get a new start in life.

Yes, the balance of power rests with those who pray.

Count on This —
God Will Work in Your Life If You Let Him
Note the Holy Boldness.

Do we hear those early disciples praying, "Now, Lord, grant unto us the tact and good sense to keep our mouths shut so as not to antagonize our captors"?

Far from it!

They asked God to

. . .Look at the situation—"behold."

...Give *them* a change of attitude—"all boldness."

...Prove his power through what they would then proceed to do—"Grant unto thy servants, that with all boldness, they may speak thy word . . . ."

What brought about this change in their lives? It was the presence and power of the Holy Spirit within them.

Initially, the Holy Spirit came to the infant church on Pentecost Day.

Constantly he assists any seeking soul who would know Christ. (John 3:5, 6). No one can become a believer without the ministry of the Holy Spirit.

He also comes to believers again and again in answer to prayer, filling and anointing them for any given task or crisis. In answer to your prayer for help, the Holy Spirit will enable you to preach or to minister or to bear a burden or to face a threat—all completely in victory. Holy boldness and the presence of the Holy Spirit are two sides of the same coin.

When the Holy Spirit is in control I have no fear of people and things around me. When the Spirit is allowed to enter every room of my heart-house, I become a changed person. Whereas before I was cringing and apologetic, now I have assurance and power.

Note the "great grace."

"With great power gave the apostles witness of the resurrection of the Lord Jesus: and great grace was upon them all." One evidence of that grace was that these early believers "were of one heart and one soul." Unity in the Body of Christ—harmony among believers—is beautifully possible when the Holy Spirit is in control.

Note the sacrifice.

Here is the crowning proof that God is doing something in the individual life.

Barnabas had some land. He sold it and brought the proceeds to the apostles, saying something like this, "Fellows, here's the money. I give it to the Lord, through you."

Does that mean that everyone who has a possession

should sell it and give the money to the church? Not at all. It does mean that when God speaks, you listen to what he asks of you, even if it means the forfeiting of some good and legitimate things you hold dear.

Sacrifice doesn't always mean giving something you can hold and handle. Sometimes it means giving *your time*. Sometimes it means giving *yourself*. Sometimes it means dropping a tear on the hand of one whose heart is breaking. Sometimes it involves your own personal heartbreak. But always, if God is working in your life, the taste of sacrifice will be sweet. To change the figure, you will have proof that God is walking in your shoes.

To sum up: We have talked about three things. First, you pick your own crowd, and the crowd you pick tells what kind of person you are. Second, in any situation—any time, anywhere—ultimate victory belongs to people who pray. And third, the real proof of the value of the years lies in what God does in your life in answer to prayer. The fullness of the Spirit, the boldness to witness, the grace of humility, the taste of sacrifice—all this, in your life, is proof of whether you got anything from God in your walk with Christ the King.

Then when you are hurt by life's harshness and you are tempted to become cynical, you can count on Christ and the certainties I have been describing.

16. Who Cares, Anyway?

You Have Some Deep Hurts, Haven't You?

... He walked off and left you with little children to raise ... Or she went to live with some other man ... Or that prodigal son abandoned your home and spent not only his money but yours too and dragged your name in the dust ... That wayward daughter stepped on your heart strings more than once ... That business associate cheated you out of thousands of dollars ... Those so-called friends or neighbors or other critics have either maliciously or ignorantly done their best to ruin you ... Oh yes, you have problems!

The Question Is: Who Cares, Anyway?

Must you just hold a firm upper lip and try to keep going somehow?

Jesus cares! He said so himself. "I am the good shepherd: the good shepherd giveth his life for the sheep" (John 10:11).

Shepherd-care—where did we hear about that before? In the 23rd Psalm, of course!

David said, "The *Lord* is my shepherd; I shall not want...." I shall not want *anything.* In God I have protection, provision, peace, refreshment, freedom from fear, calmness under pressure, hope for today and forever.... Yes, I have everything!

Someone to Depend On

Every one of us needs someone to depend on. This is a sound psychological principle. God built you to depend on him. Then sin came in and spoiled that relationship and alienated the human race from God. The prophet Isaiah, speaking for the Lord, sums up that sad situation: "Behold, the Lord's hand is not shortened that it cannot save; neither
162

his ear heavy, that it cannot hear: But your iniquities have separated between you and your God, and your sins have hid his face from you, that he will not hear" (Isaiah 59:1-2).

Sin separates us from God. But the capacity to depend on someone—to depend on *him*—is still there. What a pity that people try to quiet that yearning in so many futile ways! Pleasure, liquor, the drug scene, sex, a frantic round of activity, or whatever—none of these things can fulfill our need for a Shepherd. We never can be satisfied with anything short of God himself. There's a God-shaped vacuum in every human heart that only he can fill.

How Will I Recognize the One Who Cares?

Interestingly enough, before the Shepherd tells what he does for the sheep, he speaks of his voice. "The sheep hear his voice . . . and he leadeth them out . . . . A stranger will they not follow, but will flee from him" (John 10:3-5).

You will recognize the Shepherd by his voice. "A stranger"—now why does he bring that up? Because to have God *speak* to you through his Word is the very essence of soul satisfaction. It is all right to know that God exists, but this knowledge does not thrill your heart. It is well and good to have a grasp of Christian doctrine and be able to state what the church believes and what Christians individually should hold dear in their beliefs. It is praiseworthy to be active in Christian service and in fellowship with other Christians.

But all of these things, while good and important and necessary in their places, do not by themselves satisfy the quest of a hungering heart. No, they don't. You can be busy—but barren and lonesome and sad. You can be effective to the point of being famous and still have a heart that is unsatisfied.

Oh, hear his voice! You will recognize it if you give yourself time to hear it. Has he spoken to you today by his Word and his Holy Spirit?

How does he speak? Some portion of the Word becomes light to you. The Holy Spirit speaks directly to your heart and mind and conscience and will. He speaks through the cast of circumstances. The things that happen along life's way are calculated to bring us something right from the heart of God. They come when we wait on him.

Let us say you have read your Bible. You have said to him in prayer what you had to say. Then do take a little time just to wait in his presence. Have a little note book and write down what he says (because if you don't, you'll forget, if you're like me). If you are too busy just to spend time with the Shepherd, then in all probability you are too busy. Spend enough time to get familiar with the voice of God and you will never have trouble with the will of God.

Listening and Obeying

Let us say you have heard the Shepherd's voice through his Word. That is not enough. You will really know *him* when you start doing his will.

All of us could name a number of things we know to be the will of God for us—but we just haven't gotten around to doing anything about them. I invite you, I challenge you: Today take one of those things out of the realm of "I Ought To" and put it into the realm of "I Will." Make a list of the things that you know, beyond the shadow of a doubt, are the will of God for you. Then go to work on that list. Don't make a big issue out of it and broadcast your good intentions to your family and neighbors. Just do it! Obedience opens the way for Almightiness to work in your life.

What are some of the things we put off doing? One is forgiving; we don't like to do it. We carry around an old hurt or an old grudge. You know, forgiveness is an inside matter. It doesn't come from merely saying, "I forgive you;" the verbalization is secondary. Forgiveness has to start in the heart; too often we refuse to command our heart to let go of the strands of resentment that we have been clutching for months or perhaps years. God is saying gently, but ever so insistently, come on, forgive . . . forgive.

Did you ever fall and skin your knee, and then, after a

scab had formed over the wound, one day you found yourself picking away at it until all of a sudden the protective
layer lifted off and there was the sore, raw and bleeding
again? Oh, you say, that's a childish thing to do. Of course it
is. Well, now, stop picking at the skinned knees of your soul,
will you? Healing has to start with you and Jesus cooperat-
ing, "the love of God . . . shed abroad in your (our) hearts by
the Holy Spirit . . ." (Romans 5:5).

God's will may also involve a reorientation of your
schedule to include some minutes each day for God and his
Word. It seems such a senseless, foolish and damaging thing
to try to live a whole day without reference to the one who
can help us to live it. We endeavor to walk without benefit of
the Shepherd. It never works. "As ye have therefore received Christ Jesus the Lord, so walk ye in Him," Paul says
in Colossians 2:6. Thus living every day has to be by the
same principle that was involved when you trusted Christ as
Saviour. You received him *by faith*.

You don't live a whole day at a time. It's a step at a time, a
heartbeat at a time, one moment at a time, one dropping tear
at a time, one heartache at a time, one triumph at a time, one
chuckle at a time. Obeying God may be, on your part, so
simple a matter as just trusting God moment by moment.

Obeying God may well mean that you get down on your
knees and say, "O God, I want you to start directing me in
giving as well as living." It may well involve so simple a
thing as returning a book you've kept for years . . . or paying
back a loan that the loaner has given up ever getting back . . .
or offering an apology that you know you owe. Give some
thought today to intelligently determining what God wants
you to do.

Supply . . . Refreshment . . . Guidance

We have been looking at Psalm 23 as a commentary on
John 10. We see that Christ is the Good Shepherd of *supply*—
"green pastures . . . still waters." He is the Good Shepherd
of *refreshment*—"He restoreth my soul." He is the Good

Shepherd of *guidance*—"He leadeth me in the paths of righteousness for his name's sake."

Note the words "for his name's sake." He himself has something at stake in your life, in all that you say and do.

My father had a unique practice that pressed home this truth to my heart. When I was a teenager, and later when my father was blind, he would turn those piercing, snapping blue eyes in my direction—eyes that seemed to look right through a person—and he would say, "Remember, boy, you're carrying my name."

Well, I think our blessed Saviour looks down from the parapets of heaven and says, "Mary . . . Jim . . . Lucy . . . Joe—you bear my name. I want to guide you because my reputation is at stake."

Because of who he is, he takes care of all your needs. It's hard to believe that when you're broke; it's hard to believe when you're sick and can't lift the loads you wish you could. But look back for just a moment and, as you look over your past life, ask when the Lord failed you. When did he not supply all the *real* needs of your life? Not once! God says to us as he said to Joshua, "As I was with Moses, so will I be with thee: I will not fail thee nor forsake thee" (Joshua 1:5).

A Companion in the Valley

David said, *"Yea, though I walk through the valley . . . thou art with me."* Remember, every one goes through valleys and shadows and grief. Just because you and I call ourselves Christians does not guarantee that we will not have our share of reverses and trials and disappointments and tears. But the difference between a person who knows God through faith in Jesus Christ and one who does not know him is that the believer is never alone; the Shepherd is with him.

Think about that in terms of your own life. What, presently, are you going through? We're in days of great economic stress. Maybe your job was suddenly terminated or you were laid off for an indefinite period. Perhaps you are saying, "I wonder why the Lord let this happen to me."

We need to remind ourselves that the children of Israel, when they had passed through the Red Sea, soon encountered a good many things that must have seemed catastrophic. First there was no water. My guess is that the Lord allowed them to use the last drop in the last container, that he let them struggle with the sadness of seeing their little children whimpering for a drink of water, before he could say to them, "Now look what I am going to do for you!" Right there was Elim, with 12 wells of water and three score and ten palm trees! God allowed them to get thirsty—for a good and beneficent reason.

A little later he let them get hungry—so that he could provide for them manna, heavenly bread. Thus it is with you, too. You will never know the comfort, the rich supply of God unless you are needy. And the needier you are, the more miraculous his supply!

Let me emphasize the truth again: God purposes to lead you *through* the valley. Isaiah knew this truth when he said, "When thou passest through the waters, I will be with thee; and through the rivers, they shall not overflow thee . . . . For I am the Lord thy God, the Holy One of Israel, thy Saviour . . ." (Isaiah 43:3,2).

Here's the blessed truth that you and I should latch onto: The valley is to go *through*, not just to go *into*—and the Shepherd is there every moment.

The Psalmist speaks of the valley of the shadow *of death*. Perhaps you're in that terribly low place right now. The doctor has just told you that you, or someone you love, is suffering from an ailment for which science has no cure. How do you greet this news? If you are God's child you can honestly say, "Wonderful! God is going to take me through this." And he will! He will either perform a miracle beyond the wisdom of medical skill, or he will take you home to be "with Christ, which is far better." The real "you" is going to be around a million years from now (possessed, of course, of a resurrection body). The one who can laugh and cry and have fellowship with others is the very one whom God delights to bring eternally close to himself. Rest your heart upon it: The valley . . . of death is only a *shadow*. The Shepherd will lead you *through*.

Note the means of his aiding you. "Thy rod and thy staff they comfort me." In other words, God's discipline and God's guidance are the protection of my life and the comfort of my heart. That distinctly unpleasant and perhaps painful experience you're going through—what is the purpose of it? It is not to make you feel bad. It is to guide you. It is to make you safe in the Shepherd's presence. It is to keep you from falling off the cliff. So go through it triumphantly, because God is with you!

The Comforting One

Ours is the Good Shepherd of *comfort*. One of the most precious relationships that you and I sustain to the Saviour is one of comfort—his comforting of us. And when do you need this loving, undergirding strength? Is it when you are happiest? No, it is when happiness has flown like a bird out of the window of life, when you're lonely, or in pain, or some loved one has slipped into the gloryland and you are bereaved and hurt. Then is when you need comfort, and the Good Shepherd is there to provide it.

We have seen that this aid to our sorrowing hearts comes in two ways, by the use of the "rod" and the "staff"—the discipline of God and his protection and support. So if he is putting you through the wringer, just now, so to speak, don't fight back. Let him comfort you and guide you and enrich you through this very experience. He wants to.

We think of God as our dear Heavenly Father, and he is. But we sometimes forget *his* part of the relationship. One of the surest proofs of the Father's love for us is in his willingness to allow us to get into situations where he can comfort us.   The comfort will be perpetual; the word "presence" indicates that. Yes, there will be enemies and critics and opposition and trial. It will all be terribly real—none of it merely theoretical. There may be shortages and inabilities too great for you to meet, yourself. But, thank God, he will be there to supply everything you need!

The Gracious Host

Look at the words in verse 5: "Thou anointest my head with oil." Here the figure changes and we are given a picture of a banqueting hall. The custom in Bible lands was and still is in many countries to do something special in a personal way for an honored guest. You might take a few drops of perfumed oil and pour it on his head. Or you might anoint his feet in countries where sandals are worn and the feet become calloused and weary. The point is, *you* do something for the guest.

But here the order is reversed: *"Thou* anointest *my* head with oil." When you trust our blessed Lord as your Saviour, he turns around and honors you!

The same thought is in Revelation 3:20. You honor him when you "hear his voice and open the door and . . . sup with him." But at the same time he makes you the honored guest at his banqueting table—imagine that! God pours the holy anointing oil of his blessing upon your life every time you honor him as your Shepherd.

When you get this point of view it sanctifies every experience of your life. You will not be merely drudging through life. All of a sudden you will realize *you* are the focus of his plans.

Take a homely illustration. Hubby is bringing his boss home for dinner. All right, what do you do? Well, you go through the house like a cyclone and before long everything is clean and shining and in place. You lecture the kids about what to do and not to do. Finally the gentleman comes and you sit down to the meal. Now tell me: Who or what is the center of attention during that dinner hour? No, it is not Junior, or Sister, or Hubby and certainly not yourself. The focus is on the invited guest: Does he like his roast beef rare of does he prefer an end cut? Does he want butter or sour cream on his baked potato? Will he have sugar and cream in his coffee or does he prefer it black? You know the whole bit: *he* is the center of attention. That is as it ought to be. But have you realized, my friend, that when you trust the Lord Jesus as your Shepherd, he invests you with a singular importance. He makes *you* the focus of his plans.

Now then, when you realize that all this is true, that you are seated at God's banqueting table, that you're the honored guest, that you're the recipient of his holy planning for your life, all the events of life are seen in new perspective.

What events? Here you will have to write your own ticket, for I cannot possibly know what your circumstances are. Perhaps you have had surgery and things are not going as anticipated. You are so weak that you can scarcely get up in the morning and drag through the day. It may be you are having trouble on the job or you may be among the thousands who have been laid off. You may have lost a loved one and there is a big gaping hole in your life.

You say, "Well, Brother Cook, what in the world are you driving at? Facts are facts and I have to face them." Of course you do! But when you realize that what is happening this minute is part of the focus of God's perfect plan for your life, *you won't fight it.* You'll accept it and you'll let God use it to enrich your life.

Look, now: When did he speak of the anointing with oil? When did the concept of being the honored guest come? These precious words came after "the valley of the shadow of death," after the presence of opposition and enemies. That's the time that you become aware of being God's honored guest. That's the point at which you look up and say, "Lord, I know you care about me. I'm someone unique and special in your eyes. You attention is focused upon me and your lovely plans are being worked out—whether I can see it all now or not."

The Overflowing Cup
Next we have the blessed concept of the overflowing cup. "My cup runneth over." Do you know anything exper-

ientially about this truth? If you don't—and you'd like to—here's how to begin: Just wait with your Lord long enough so that he *can* fill you.

Let us suppose you are at a picnic and you're in a long line at the serving table. You've helped yourself to a piece of barbecued chicken and an ear of corn and a serving of potato salad. You're steadying your plastic knife and fork and spoon and your napkin with your third finger underneath. Now you want a beverage to go with this good meal and you pick cup an empty plastic up and move forward in the line.

As you look ahead to the business end of that long line you see somebody tipping the container so that the last few drops of liquid come out of the spigot. You think: Oh, boy! They've run out! So you leave the line.

What you don't know is that there are five or six other containers under the counter, ready to be lifted into place as they are needed. But you have walked away disappointed and perhaps even disgusted—to eat your chicken and corn and potato salad with nothing to wash them down. Well, you should have stayed in line, shouldn't you?

This kind of thing happens to us all the time, in a spiritual sense. We say our prayers, morning or night, and we rush away. We ought to stay in line a little longer so that God can fill up the empty cup of our needy lives.

Those of you who have lived in the Chicago area may remember a chain of restaurants that advertised "the bottomless cup." When you dined there and your coffee cup was not even half empty, a waitress would come around and fill it right up again—with no extra charge to you. I like that!

"Cup" speaks of enjoyment, of the savoring of a piquant good taste. So, applying the figure to yourself, you can say, "I'm enjoying myself to the full—and this good feeling just doesn't quit!" But you have to stay in line, so to speak, long enough for him to fill your cup.

You're reading your Bible, are you? Spend three, or four or five minutes longer turning the truth over slowly in your mind. You're praying, are you? Remain on your knees a few more minutes. Most of us stop far too soon. Oh, see for yourself the delight that God pours into your life when you stay with him those extra moments. If you will do this, you will be amazed at the direction he gives, the guidance he provides, the correction he points to. The waiting precedes the overflowing—don't miss it.

To be more specific, just how do you come by this overflowing life? There are three ingredients that must be taken together.

First, the *Word of God*—you get it into your mind. Second, the *will of God*—you specialize in finding it and doing it. Third, the *work of God*—you share your Saviour with other people because you're so excited about him yourself.

The overflowing life is a by-product of something the Lord does for you when you let him. You don't *try* to overflow any more than a half-filled glass of water can try to fill itself beyond its brim. Let us look separately at the three ingredients which, taken together, produce a blessed overflow in the Christian life.

The only thing that will permanently modify human behavior is the infusion of large amounts of the Word of God into the mind and heart. Too often we read the Bible routinely, to put a little salve on our consciences.

How should you treat the Bible? Read it, think about it, pray over it, memorize a portion of it, and meditate on that portion all day long. Thus you store the Word of God in your unconscious mind, which is the computer portion of your thinking apparatus so that the Holy Spirit can bring out that portion of Scripture when you need it. We are talking about the overflowing life and I can tell you this: The blessing that comes *from* your life is in direct proportion to the Word of God that gets *into* your life.

Someone told me about a friend who wanted to quit smoking. It so happened that about the time this determination took hold of him, he learned about the procedure we have been talking about concerning the storing up of the Word of God in the heart. That is, reading it, thinking about it, memorizing a portion of it, and mulling over that portion all day.

He was working on the 10th chapter of First Corinthians where there is the verse that reads: "There hath no temptation taken you but such as is common to man: But God is faithful, who will not suffer you to be tempted above that ye are able: but will with the temptation also make a way of escape, that ye may be able to bear it" (v. 13). That was the verse that he was putting into all the little empty places of the day as he meditated upon it.

It so happened that one night after dinner a great craving for a smoke came over him. He didn't have any on him, so he started to go to the corner store to get a pack. The walk would give opportunity for him to repeat "his verse," as he had been doing at odd moments all day. He said it once. And again.

He stopped. "If that verse is true, why am I going to the store for cigarettes?", he asked himself. Then, "God, if your Word is true, why am I doing this? I don't have to do this. It says so."

He turned and went home—and never picked up a cigarette again. You see, because the Word of God was in his heart, he had been enabled to plug his faith into the switchboard of heaven. The message of victory came out loud and clear!

We have been talking about the overflowing life, and we have seen that the first necessity is the saturation of mind and heart with the Word of God. Now comes attention to the *will of God.* Our Saviour could say, "I delight to do thy will, O my God." Do you know the thrill, the sheer delight of knowing you're doing what God wants done? My brothers and sisters, try one entire day in which you ask, before you do anything, "What does God want done about this?"

Perhaps you are in school. You have homework to do, activities to engage in. Why not say, "Lord, help me to do this the way you want it done?" I'll guarantee things will go better, your mind will be clearer than if you hadn't given those few minutes to the Lord. God doesn't want you to just get by. He wants you to do well. "Whatsoever ye do, do it heartily, as to the Lord, and not unto men" (Colossians 3:23). That's his will for you.

Or it may be you are a businessman with large responsibilities. You are told to carve $100,000 from the advertising budget. Are you going to cut straight across the board and say, "I can't help it; that's the way it is"? No, you use all the discretion you can summon. You find out which part of the operation can be omitted without harm to the whole. Why not admit the incompleteness of your knowledge and say, "Lord, what do you want done here?"

Oh, what delight there is in learning the will of God and *doing* it—whether it is pushing a pencil, or ironing clothes, or washing the floor, or selling a used car, or making a call as a traveling salesman, or working as a physician or surgeon or anesthetist or nurse, or trying a case as an attorney, or doing any one of the many other tasks that cannot be easily categorized. Do you know the kind of delight that comes from doing the will of God all day long? It is part of the overflowing life.

We have spoken of the Word of God and the will of God as being components of the overflowing life. There follows, naturally and logically, the work of God—the enablement to introduce others to the Lord Jesus Christ. Jesus said, "Ye have not chosen me, but I have chosen you, and ordained you, that ye should go and bring forth fruit . . ." (John 15:16). Fruit-bearing means winning others to Jesus. The joy of sharing *his* life with others will fill your cup to overflowing.

What is the "fruit" of a Christian? It is more Christians, of course, just as the fruit of an apple is more apple trees and the fruit of a grain of wheat is more wheat.

We are inclined to make hard work of so-called witnessing. It is not accomplished by our *doing* anything; it comes from our absorbing something—and that something, as we have seen, is the Word of God. Soul-winning comes from the overflow of enthusiasm, and it becomes as natural for you to speak of the Lord you love (if you really do know and love him) as it is for a boy to talk about his Honda, or a girl to discuss her new boyfriend, or a housewife to speak of her new diet, or a businessman to speak of a new stock that is paying extra high dividends. You talk about things you are excited about, isn't that true?

I'm a gadget man. I saw this new flashlight, different from any I had ever seen before. It was skillfully engineered, well turned out. So I bought it.

I put the flashlight on the front seat of my car, and when I stopped to talk with someone I reached over with my right hand and picked up that new flashlight and said, "Hey, did you ever see one like this?"

My friend held it in his hand for a moment. "That's sure a dandy!" he said—and we talked about flashlights.

There was no speech, no contrived approach. Here was Cook, delighted over something he'd gotten, eager to tell his buddy about it. I think our trouble in soul-winning is that we're not very excited about Jesus some of the time—or much of the time, or even maybe all the time.

Can you speak of your Lord naturally, without getting a pious tremor in your voice? An atheist said to me many years ago, "Cook, your voice tone changes when you talk about your Jesus." He didn't mean this as a compliment. He was putting his finger on a lack of genuineness in me. From that moment I determined that when I speak of my Lord I would be reverent, yes; but I would also be as genuine and honest as I want to be when I am talking about any one or anything else.

But I *will* speak for him. This is part of the overflowing life. Old Dr. Trumbull had a good rule. He said, "Whenever I am justified in choosing the subject of conversation, I will endeavor to speak of my blessed Lord and win my friend to him." (There are some times when you don't have any right to intrude your thoughts into a conversation. You'll know when those times occur; the Holy Spirit will guide you.) Let Jesus do something precious in your own life so that you can share him with an air of discovery and excitement like Andrew's when he exclaimed, "We have found the Messiah, which is . . . the Christ" (John 1:41).

These, then, are the components of the overflowing life:

God's Word—in you, God's will—for you, God's work—
through you.

Giver of Goodness and Mercy

Notice the next words: "Surely goodness and mercy shall
follow me all the days of my life." What do "goodness" and
"mercy" mean in terms of the shepherding ministry of the
Lord Jesus Christ?

The kind of goodness that God *is* and that he imparts is
never saccharine sweet, with emphasis only on love. One of
the great needs of our day is a resurgence of the truths of
holiness and righteousness which are as much a part of the
divine nature as love is.

Isaiah, that majestic prophet who foretold in so many
ways the coming of the Lord Jesus Christ, himself had a
mighty experience of the holiness of God. This is how he
speaks of it:

> In the year that king Uzziah died I saw also
> the Lord sitting upon a throne, high and lift-
> ed up ... Above it stood the seraphim ...
> And one cried unto another, and said, Holy,
> holy, holy, is the Lord of hosts: the whole
> earth is full of his glory. And the posts of the
> door moved at the voice of him that cried,
> and the house was filled with smoke. Then
> said I, Woe is me! for I am undone; because I
> am a man of unclean lips ... for mine eyes
> have seen the King, the Lord of hosts (Isaiah
> 6:1-5).

In the days of the Puritans and other old-timers, there
was great emphasis on the holiness of God with little time
spent in extolling his love. Today we have swung to the
opposite direction. We laud the love of God with almost
complete exclusion of the righteousness of his nature and his
dealings. The shepherding work of the Lord Jesus Christ is
to reveal him in *both* aspects of holiness and love. What does
such a view of God do for you?

First, when you live your life in the atmosphere of this kind of divine goodness, your own attitudes toward right and wrong are profoundly affected. Most of us want our own way—or else!

My good friend, Dr. Clyde Narramore, tells of this incident. His daughter is now a charming young lady and college graduate, but at the time of this story she was a very small child who had done something that needed correction. Her psychologist father invited her gently, "Come sit on my lap and let's talk about this."

She did sit on his knee, all right. But she put a little chubby arm around his neck and whispered in his ear, "Daddy, let's not talk it over. Let's let me have my way." How like her we are!

Second, this understanding of God's true goodness will enable you to look at all the events of your life in the context of God's perfect plan for you—and I do mean all! He is the *Good* Shepherd. To his own, "all things work together *for good.*" When we grasp that truth, the things that "happen" to you and me are now received from the viewpoint of God's goodness. I'll tell you something, friends: That realization will take all the pressure out of situations that are frustrating you or breaking your heart!

And third, depending upon how close your relationship with the Shepherd is, you will project his goodness to other people. "That the love wherewith thou hast loved me," Jesus prayed, "may be in them and I in them" (John 17:26).

Look at this second word, "mercy." Ours is a holy God, but he is also a God of mercy. He makes provisions for our failures. The Apostle John put it this way in the second chapter of his first letter: "My little children, these things write I unto you, that ye sin not"—that is, you are not to make a practice of sinning. You do not need to fall prey to temptation, for Jesus died and rose again to keep you.

But you are a human being, prone to stumble. When this occurs, what then? "We have an advocate with the Father," John says, "Jesus Christ the righteous." Your Shepherd is not only the holy God manifesting himself to you, but he is also the holy God loving you enough to pick you up when you fall down, dust you off, and get you started again.

I am glad for that, aren't you? Christ is the Shepherd who manifests the holiness of God until we tremble in awe before his sheer shining perfection, but who also reaches out his nail-pierced hand and says, "Come to me. I died for you. I paid for your sins. I love you."

> He waiteth not for penitence
> But hasteth to begin
> The restoration of a saint
> The instant of his sin.

So you see, there's a dynamic tension here between the holiness of God that says you must not trifle with sin, and the compassion and love of God that says, "I love you because you're a human being and I'm going to stick with you and get you home to heaven."

The Way to the Father's House

The culmination of the Shepherd's care is his provision of the heavenly home. "I will dwell in the house of the Lord forever." Yes, he will guide you today and tomorrow and all the days until you are safe home at last, sharing his nearness. These are Jesus' words (though not in the familiar sequence):

> Let not your heart be troubled . . . trust in me.
> There are many homes up there where my
> Father lives, and I am going to prepare them
> for your coming. When everything is ready,
> then I will come and get you, so that you can
> always be with me where I am . . . (John 14:1-3
> *Living Bible*).

What is your present relation to the Shepherd? Are you hearing his voice in your innermost soul? Are you seeking his will and finding joy in following it? Are you drinking deeply of his comfort and his grace? Are you reaching out to other lives because your own "cup" overflows?

Perhaps you have never come to him at all, as a sinner to the Saviour. He himself has said, ". . . him that cometh to me I will in no wise cast out" (John 6:37b). He will give you a place in his flock (Psalms 77:20a), in his family (John 1:12), in his heart of love (Jeremiah 31:3).

Thank God for this Shepherd! He cares—he *really* cares for you, now and for eternity. He is "for real." You can be, too.

17. Are You for Real?

Two girls left a youth meeting together. They had just heard the message of a visiting minister who enjoyed considerable popularity.

"Boy!" one of the girls exclaimed. "Wasn't he *great*?"

There was a pause. "Yes, if you think so," her friend replied. "But that man couldn't tell me one thing. He talks about kindness; but what does he do? When he was invited to speak to our group last year he didn't show up, and he's never apologized. He talks about honesty, but he latches on to anybody else's literary efforts that appeal to him without so much as a word of credit. . . . So far as I'm concerned, he's a phony."

Perhaps the charges are unreasonable. But they're the kind that are leveled every day against Christians by individuals who want to know the true relation between *belief* (that we say we have) and *behavior* (that we display), between *faith* and *conduct*. People want to know: are we for real?

The book of James has a good deal to say on this subject. We need to read several verses and look at them carefully. James says:

> What doth it profit, my brethren, though a man say he hath faith, and have not works? Can faith save him? If a brother or sister be naked, and destitute of daily food, and one of you say unto them, Depart in peace, be ye warmed and filled; notwithstanding, ye give them not those things which are needful to the body, what doth it profit?

Even so faith, if it hath not works, is dead, being alone. Yea, a man may say, Thou hast faith, and I have works; show me thy faith without thy works, and I will show thee my faith by my works. Thou believest that there is one God; thou doest well: the devils also believe and tremble. But wilt thou know, O vain man, that faith without works is dead? Was not Abraham our father justified by works, when he had offered Isaac his son upon the altar? Seest thou how faith wrought with his works, and by works was faith made perfect?

And the Scripture was fulfilled which saith, Abraham believed God, and it was imputed unto him for righteousness: and he was called the Friend of God. Ye see then how that by works a man is justified, and not by faith only. Likewise also was not Rahab the harlot justified by works, when she had received the messengers, and had sent them out another way? For as the body without the spirit is dead, so faith without works is dead also (James 2:14-26).

At first glance James, with his insistence upon works, seems to be in conflict with Paul whose emphasis is on salvation by grace alone, through faith, apart from works.

A closer look, however, shows that these two writers complement each other perfectly. The passage we have just read turns on the phrase, "I will *show* thee my faith by my works."

The evidence of what you really are in heart commitment to God will show up in what you do. Your conduct is a perfect mirror of your heart attitude toward God. Its expression is automatic ... it is inevitable ... it is unchanging—sharply distinguished from mere words.

A man may say, "I have faith," but James retorts, "Show me!"

What we say doesn't always reveal what we are down deep in our hearts. Psychiatrists and psychologists tell us that when a person comes to them with a problem, this is generally called the "presenting" complaint or set of symptoms. The doctors use this phrase because so very often, the real problem is something else. You always look for the problem underneath the problem, and you search for the complaint behind the complaint, they say. Speech may couch a profession of something that neither the heart nor the conduct possesses.

The commitment of faith and the evidence of conduct are tied together. Scripture shows this union. I'll give you a few instances: Romans 10:9: "Confess with thy mouth . . . believe in thine heart." Again, a verse which is often quoted to encourage people to trust Christ for salvation: "By grace are ye saved through faith; and that not of yourselves: it is the gift of God: not of works, lest any man should boast. For we are his workmanship, created in Christ Jesus unto good works, which God hath before ordained that we should walk in them" (Ephesians 2:8-10). Thus we see that faith and grace and salvation and good works are all tied together in the same package.

This truth, in a negative sense, is given to us by our Lord Jesus as recorded in Mark 7:21: "For from within, out of the heart of men, proceed evil thoughts, adulteries, fornications, murders, thefts, covetousness, wickedness, deceit, lasciviousness, an evil eye, blasphemy, pride, foolishness. All these evil things come from within, and defile the man." Real faith, real commitment in my heart to God, and proper conduct in line with that commitment are inseparable.

Incidentally, *vague mental assent to belief in God does no good whatsoever.* Even demons "believe" in that sense. "Thou believest there is one God; . . . the devils also believe, and tremble" (James 2:19). Tremble is our word for "shudder." The servants of Satan shudder when they think of what it means to be responsible to a holy God.

I've noticed that is it possible for us to become quite righteous in our attitude when someone questions us about our relation to Christ, especially when we are in a so-called "Christian" community. We stand up straight and say, "Of course I'm a Christian!" In that, we are like the Pharisees of old who said, "We are Abraham's children, and were never in bondage . . . ." They were in bondage that minute and the Lord knew it! Not only were they under the heel of Rome, but they were also held slaves by their own sins. Yet no one likes to have his spiritual state scrutinized.

I didn't realize how much I was annoying some members of my congregation in Glen Ellyn, Illinois, years ago by asking them, when they went out of the church on Sunday morning, "How is it with you? How is it with your soul? How are things going with you, John? . . . Mary?"

One day someone had enough courage to tell me, "You know, Pastor, you offend me by asking, 'How are things with you?' That's *my* business."

"Well," I replied, "it's also mine, as an undershepherd of God's flock."

We get sensitive when someone asks, "How's your prayer life?" We recoil and say, "Look—I pray, regularly!" But that self-righteous stance doesn't prove a thing. It may only reveal that our lives are shallow spiritually and in need of some overhauling.

How, then, do you show people, if you wish to, that you are actually *real* with God?

Well, to begin with, you don't go around trying to prove that you are spiritually okay. There is no one, I think, so odious as a person whose main goal is to make you think he is spiritually superior to others.

The Bible gives a twofold test for realness.

The proof that you are real with God comes, I think, as a by-product of two attitudes of heart that James speaks of.

First, is there readiness to give God one's most treasured possession?

At this point James gives an illustration from the life of Abraham. Abraham was a fine man. He held the exalted title of "a friend of God." Although he made a few mistakes in his lifetime, generally speaking his character was impeccable. His attitude toward God was consistently right. In relation to God, he was one of the greatest figures in all of the history of the human race.

Well, James said, there came a time when Abraham had to prove to the people in the culture around him that this faith in God was real. This proof required that he—Abraham—be willing to take his most precious possession and say, "Okay, God—you can have him."

Now in Abraham's case it was Isaac who was to be "given." Abraham was 100 years old when Isaac was born—a biological miracle in itself, for Sarah was beyond the age of childbearing.

Years before Isaac's birth, as Abraham saw time passing with no likelihood of his having an heir, this father tried to "help God out." So he had a child by Hagar, his servant girl, a course of action that was never accepted as part of God's plan and provision. Abraham had his troubles with Ishmael, the son of that union. To this day the descendants of Ishmael are a thorn in the side of God's chosen people, as you know. At least they are considered so by the descendants of Abraham.

Now Isaac is born, and I suppose every time Abraham looks at Isaac he says, "There—in this boy—is the fulfillment of God's promise, 'In Isaac shall thy seed be called. Your descendants are going to come through Isaac, Abraham.'"

How infinitely precious that son must have been to Abraham! He was the miracle child of his old age. But more than that, he was the *only* means, so far as Abraham knew, of God's fulfillment of his word.

It is against this background that we see the picture in Genesis 22:1,2: "And it came to pass . . . that God did tempt (test) Abraham, and said unto him, Abraham: and he said, Behold, here I am. And he said, Take now thy son, thine only son Isaac, whom thou lovest, and . . . offer him for a burnt offering upon one of the mountains which I will tell thee of."

When I read this portion the other day I thought, if I were Abraham, I would have said, "Lord, I don't think I heard you just right. Would you mind repeating that last sentence? . . . You don't mean *me*, Lord—that I am to do this? . . . You don't mean Isaac?"

"Yes, I mean you, Abraham. And I mean offer Isaac."

"You mean, offer him as a *sac*—" Abraham could not complete the word that cut his own heart. Finally, "You mean offer Isaac as a sacrifice the same way that I offer other sacrifices?"

That's unthinkable, Abraham must have reasoned. And yet God tested him this way because this was *the* test of whether Abraham had real faith.

How does all this relate to you and me? I have no way of knowing what is most precious to you. I think those things change as the years go by, or at least our evaluation of them changes. But it is highly possible for you to get some testing, today, along the line of *things* that are very dear to you now: things that involve your culture, your lifestyle, your music; things that relate to sex, to money, or to one of many other categories.

I had a man in a church once who got angry every time I mentioned tithing. Why? Because this subject touched him where he hurt. I finally lost him. I missed that $10.00 he put in the offering plate every Sunday (he would have been giving $100.00 if he had been a tither). Money was a precious thing to him.

No, I can't tell you what it is that is most precious to you. But I can tell you this: If you want people to believe in your Jesus, you'd better take that thing or that person who is most precious to you—that comes closest to the quick of your soul—and hand that over to God, because if you don't, people won't believe you are for real.

The reason folks aren't lining up to get into churches today is that they don't think we Christians are genuine. Oh, they know we parrot the lingo all right, but they don't think we're honest—and most of the time, they're right!

Now, in addition to Abraham, who was asked to give

God his most precious possession as an illustration of real faith, James offers another example. He seems to be saying here:

In the second place, is there willingness to give God yourself—your whole person?

This test involved a person of entirely different character and background to those of Abraham. Rahab was a prostitute. She lived on the city wall, a place of easy access; everybody knew her. Came the spies . . . she received them . . . she evidenced the fact that she believed their God was *the* God, Jehovah God, and she said, "Promise me that when you come again (I know you will conquer this city), promise me that you will spare my family." And they said, "We'll do it." They gave her the signal that she should have the scarlet cord in the window of her house.

What about Rahab? You certainly couldn't say that her faith was evidenced by her lifestyle. If she came in and sat down in our congregation today, she might find a couple of chairs on either side of her—empty. So her lifestyle didn't prove that she was any good to God or to people. What made her decision of such great importance that it is included in the sacred Scriptures?

James says, "Was not Rahab the harlot justified by works, when she had received the messengers, and had sent them out another way?" In other words, when she was face to face with the fact that God is *God*, and that he is going to get his will done, she took her life and handed it over to him! She said in effect, "I believe you enough that you can have my life."

Note the contrast: Abraham was a good person, and he had to give the most precious thing in the world to him. Rahab was a bad person (by our moral standards), but God said, 'I'll take what you offer me—yourself."

Have you thought recently about the difference between people? We have lots of indices that we use in classifying our peers: an appealing personality . . . a person who looks "sharp" . . . who smells nice . . . who has a certain acceptable set of rules for conduct. Of course, anyone who likes *me* is a pretty fine person—you know that.

Have you thought about the fact that God says that after you do the best you can, and when you have sprinkled that "best" all over with Chanel No. 5, you still smell bad to him? All of our righteousness are as filthy rags. Jesus said to his disciples, "When ye have done *all* these things (that's everything that God has commanded you), say, we are unprofitable servants." Has it ever occurred to you that after you have done your best, it still takes a miracle to make you any good to God?

Rahab was the embodiment of this kind of divine working in a human heart. She is mentioned not only here in the book of James but also in Hebrews 11 among the heroes of faith—so in very truth, she was for real! The miracle of God's grace took place when this unworthy woman risked everything, her life and future—all that she was—on God.

I think people look to see whether our faith in God is great enough to affect our basic commitment with the peripheral precautions that we put around us. To sing, "I surrender all" is one thing; to be willing to surrender *all* is quite another thing!

In your own life, how perfectly is the will of God displayed in the events that make up your day? You don't live life as a package to be received. You live life in the same way that you break pieces off a loaf, one at a time.

Let's talk about students for a moment, although these truths are not peculiar to any one category of endeavor.

Take any given day in the life of a student. What happens? The alarm goes off. You use three words: "Good morning, Lord" or "Good Lord, morning!" In either case you have to get up. You either get up in time for breakfast, or you sleep longer and make it to your first class without food, hoping you can cut chapel or have an early lunch or have a candy bar on your way somewhere.

You go to class. You are either successful or unsuccessful, depending on whether you have studied and whether, upon studying, you have retained anything. You greet your friends, you snub your enemies. You have lunch (and comment on it). You go on through the rest of your classes and to the end of the day. Finally, it's half past midnight and you think, man, I've got to hit the sack or I'll be dead tomorrow. So you close your eyes and if you pray you say, "Well, goodnight, Lord. Take care of everything until morning."

You haven't done anything wrong. You haven't gone out with any other man's wife (or husband). You haven't stolen anything. So, you think, you're not such a bad sort.

However, if you grant that all of us are equal at Calvary, if you agree that the best of us as well as the worst of us deserve only hell and judgment except for the grace of God, then I submit to you that an ordinary day, such as the one we've related to student life, hasn't proved anything to anybody, has it? You have lived through your day, professing to be a Christian but living a pretty ordinary life on a secular level.

You want people to believe that you are real, don't you? Then you'd better live your life, step by step and moment by moment, in honest abandonment to Jesus Christ. When you start the day, talk to him. When you enter into any given situation (classroom, workshop, home, whatever) commit it to him. When you have opportunity for conversation with someone else, whisper a prayer that God will talk through your throat and look through your eyes. When you are in athletic competition, when you are on a date, when you are just relaxing for a while, commit that process to God. In so doing you cast your whole *life* upon him, segment by segment. And what happens? You prove to other people that he's real . . . that he will never let you down. And you prove also that *you* are real.

Abraham yielded to God his most precious possession.

Rahab risked her whole life on God.

If you want people to want your Jesus, James says you must go and do likewise. There is no other way. Jesus calls on you to walk the high road—the road that helps you reach for greatness.

18. What Great Things Are You Reaching For?

If you are like me, every now and then you feel sharp pricks of desire for progress in some area or other of your life. You long to move forward, to register growth, to experience something really worthwhile issuing from the smallness of the moment. Right?

If such progress is possible—and I believe it is—we ought to be able to find "how-to" illustrations for attaining it in the Word of God. And we do.

The Lord himself holds out the prospect of "greater things" for his followers. He told this first to Nathanael. He tells it to us as well.

Get the picture, sketched in John's Gospel (1:43-50). Philip had heard Jesus' call, "Follow me," and had obeyed. Immediately he went to look up Nathanael. When he located him, Philip shouted, "We have *found* him . . . of whom Moses did write . . . Jesus of Nazareth!"

Nathanael was nonplussed at this news. "Nazareth?" he questioned. "That slum? Why, there even the garbage man lives out of town. Can any good thing come out of *Nazareth?*" But Nathanael got moving.

When Jesus saw Nathanael coming to him, he said of him. "Behold an Israelite indeed in whom is no guile." And Nathanael, with the unconscious naïveté of his own self-esteem, exclaimed, "How do you know about *me*?"

"Oh," the Lord answered, "before Philip called you, you were sitting under a fig tree. I saw you."

Well, this display of omniscience was too much for Nathanael. He was down on his knees in a twinkling. "Rabbi!" he breathed. "Thou art the Son of God. Thou art the King of Israel."

Notice the answer the Lord gave him: "Because I said I

saw thee under the fig tree, believest thou? Thou shalt see greater things than these."

I want to lift out of that verse just these words:

"Believest thou? Thou shalt see *greater things* than these."

Here is a foolproof formula for spiritual progress. Want some "greater things" in your own life? Here are steps you can take, all of them recorded in John's Gospel.

Step One—Hand Yourself Over

"Believe." This word, as Greek scholars will tell you, is a rich concept that means commit yourself entirely to, without reservation, in the sense of complete surrender. That's what the Bible means when it says, "Believe on the Lord Jesus Christ." The Latins have a beautiful word for that, *entregar,* which means "hand yourself over."

Have you indeed handed yourself over to God?

"Well, then," said our Lord to Nathanael and he says it also to us, " 'thou shalt see greater things.' "

What are some of these "greater things"? Let me tick off a few of them as we find them in various chapters of the Gospel of John.

Greater Confidence

John 2 contains a couple of points for our attention. One is that when you hand yourself over to the Lord Jesus, He gives you the best even after the wine of life has run out.

What a horrible nightmare it would be to run out of refreshments at a wedding reception! You've said to the people that their presence was requested. They have come. At this very moment they are at the reception table. You have to face them. "We're sorry," you say. "We're all out of hors d'oeuvres. Please leave your present at the door . . . and go." How unthinkable!

Something just like this happened at a wedding in Cana. The mother of our Lord said to him, "They have run out."

Jesus countered with, "My hour is not yet come."

But see what the sublime faith of one who *knew* could do. That baby boy, of whom the angel had told this woman years before, now grown to be a man of 30 years, was no ordinary man. He was Messiah. Mary was sure of that.

With confident shining face she said to the servants, "Whatsoever he says to you, do it."

You know the story. Jesus commanded the servants to fill the water jars with water and (when this was done) to take some of the contents and give it to the toastmaster of the reception. In surprise that person exclaimed, "Everybody usually gives his best to the guests first, but you've kept the best until the last!"

What does this narrative say to us? Simply this: Whoever hands himself over to Christ, in absolute abandonment to him, will find growing within him a great confidence that God will always give his *best*.

An evangelist friend of mine told this story in a public meeting so I assume it is all right for me to repeat it. He said that when he was a student at a certain college he was desperately in love with a girl who wouldn't even look at him.

He prayed, "O Lord, make her notice me." But nothing happened. She wouldn't even give him the time of day.

Finally, in utter misery, he transferred to another college. And as things go, he fell in love with another girl and married her. In the twenty-some happy years that followed, he became a successful evangelist.

Now, as he told the story, he said that he was in a series of meetings in the South—one of those arrangements whereby the speaker is housed in somebody's home and has his meals in the homes of various ones of the congregation.

One day the host pastor said to the evangelist, "We're having lunch today at Mr. and Mrs. So-and-so's house. She says she went to school with you."

"Oh," my friend replied, "I don't remember going to school with anybody by that name."

"Well," the pastor said, "her maiden name was Thus-and-thus."

Like a thunderclap the truth shook him: That was the girl he had been so deeply in love with in college days.

He thought: "O God, do I have to open those old wounds? Do I have to go through all that suffering again—relive that painful memory?"

As much as he could, he dragged his feet. But eventually they arrived at the friends' house. The master greeted them cordially, at the same time saying, "I want you to meet my wife."

"Well," said my evangelist friend as he related the story, "I took one look at her and my heart began to sing 'Praise God from whom all blessings flow.' I don't know whether her own theme song was 'Deep and Wide,' but as we faced each other and I remembered the happiness of my married life, I realized that God had given the *best* to me after all."

God always gives the best, if you leave the choice to him. The sad thing is that we insist on our own choices, and then we have time—often a long, long time—to wish it had been otherwise. Don't blow your opportunity for a life that matters in eternal terms by insisting on having your own way.

"Believest thou?" Have you turned yourself over to God? Really? Then you can surely know he gives the *best*.

Greater Perception

There's another point in that second chapter of John that emphasizes "greater things." It has to do with leadership. Our Lord Jesus went into the temple and found people buying and selling there. He formed a whip of small cords and physically drove them out. After the initial shock of that experience was over, the onlookers asked the inevitable question, "Who do you think you are?"

The Bible puts it in these words: "What sign showest thou unto us, seeing that thou doest these things?" Literally, "What right have you to order us around?"

Jesus answered, "Destroy this temple, and in three days I will raise it up . . . . But he spake of the temple of his body." (His disciples remembered that saying after he was risen from the dead.)

In effect the Lord Jesus was saying, "You ought to know

what claim I have to leadership. I'm a specialist in resurrection. That's why."

Now bring this concept into 20-century thinking and you will realize that the only person who has any true right to leadership is one who is so full of the risen Christ that his power is projected into every relationship of life.

You and I are not simply to be religious from time to time, while on other occasions we are engaged in being secularly successful. Rather, our claim to leadership has to be based on something far "greater": that Jesus Christ is alive; that he is alive *today*, and that by the Holy Spirit he walks in *my* shoes, sees through *my* eyes, talks through *my* mouth—when I yield my body to him.

Therein is the claim (and the only claim, I remind you) that any of us has on another person's attention. Right here may be the reason that people don't follow you. It is because they don't find in you that divine reason for following. Get this: "greater things" not only may be, but also *must* be evident in our lives, the product of the presence and power of the living Christ in us.

Greater Comprehension

The "greater things" that we have been talking about are, incidentally, the answer to doubts and doubters, as the conversation of Jesus and Nicodemus reveals. This statement is an over-simplification, obviously, for there are many honest intellectual questions that face each of us. There is no substitute for doing your homework in thinking through the knotty intellectual issues that all of us must grapple with in the process of growing up.

The fact remains, however, that about 90 percent of our difficulty in facing up to the will of God comes, not because we cannot *think* about it, but because we do not *wish to accept it*. When I say a big *yes* to God's will and God himself in my life, surprisingly my intellectual difficulties seem to vanish. Christ is the answer.

Where do I get this idea? From John 3. Jesus said to

Nicodemus, "Marvel not that I said unto you, Ye must be born again." Nicodemus was stumbling over what he thought was a biological impossibility. The Lord Jesus said, "Look. I built the universe and keep it operating on split-second timing. I also engineered your body, that incredibly complex system of cells that keeps you functioning as a person. *I* am the one who is telling you that you need a new nature and new birth from above."

Yes, ask your questions. Yes, search for answers. But when you come to the end of it all, look up and say, "Lord, what wilt thou have me to do?" I guarantee that many of the stubborn questions you wrestled with, that (unknown to you at the time) had their genesis in your will rather than in your intellect, will be fully satisfied.

Greater Communication

I submit to you that the story of chapter 4 of John's Gospel, far from being a focus on the Samaritan woman with her checkered and indiscriminate past (she loved not wisely but too well), points up rather what the Lord Jesus did with her relationship with people.

When she arrived at Jacob's ancient well, she had that gleam in her eye. Although the Bible doesn't say this, I am sure that this lady who wasn't a lady, having a somewhat sophisticated background, was thinking, "Why is this Jewish man speaking to me at all? . . . unless it is for the oldest reason in the world. Is this a proposition?"

She waited there long enough, and listened intently enough to learn that the one who spoke to her was indeed the Son of God, the Messiah. Leaving her water jar on the stone coping of the well, she hurried back into the town and said to the men, "Come see a man who told me all whatsoever I did."

And did they ever come! (You can't tell a man who has been indiscreet that someone has told on him without producing some excitement.) They heard the woman's story. It was not what they had expected. They saw the Son of God.

"Now," they said, "we believe, not by thy saying only but because we have seen and heard for ourselves."

You see, Jesus gave this woman a different reason for communicating with other people.

We talk about witnessing. We speak of it as though it were a chore, or a duty to be done. It *is* a duty; our Lord said, "Ye shall be witnesses unto me." But witnessing, at its normal best, is a byproduct of excitement about the Lord Jesus Christ.

The problem with many a person who tries to talk about Jesus is that he or she is just a little bit embarrassed about Christ. Not excited but embarrassed, trying somehow to bootleg the concept of heaven in the side door of the conversation rather than thrillingly approaching with: "I met somebody and he made a big difference in my life!"

"Ye shall see greater things," Jesus said—among them a different and a greater reason for communicating with people. As a Christian, the victorious, transforming, risen Christ is the underlying reason for my talking to anybody, any time.

Greater Acceptance

Chapter 5 of John's Gospel shows a state of mind that most of us have known full well at one time or another. If you have not reached that point, you doubtless will some time —the point at which you feel nobody cares and nobody can help you. When you try to help yourself somebody else always gets ahead of you. Life has such situations, and when you get there the bitterness and the frustration and the hopelessness will almost overwhelm you. Read the story of the impotent man (John 5:1-9). Think what it must have meant to have had a total stranger look down and say, "Would you like to be well?"

The word of healing was spoken at the moment of deepest frustration. "Come on," Jesus said. "Roll up your pallet and be on your way."

If you have given yourself to Jesus Christ in the sense of

the word "believe" (handing yourself over), then, when you get to the end of your capacity and of your ability, when you are at the point of total frustration, thank God, Jesus is *there*. Standing over you in that moment when you cannot do a thing but groan in your powerlessness is the Son of God. He says, "Come on, there's a step you can take. Now take it." Accept his word and obey it!

Let me go back, now, to the verse that started us. "Believest thou? Thou shalt see greater things." Believe—hand yourself over to God. For some of us this still is not done. There are secret pockets of resistance: some hang-up, some deep resentment, some festering hurt, some overpowering desire to have our own way.

Oh, let us hand ourselves over completely to God. When we do, "the future is as bright as the promises of God." The "greater things" are not only *there*, but they are there for us. That is what will make the United States a great nation in the eyes of God.

19. USA: Rejoice, Repent, Resolve!

The United State of America has much to rejoice about. Our growth and prosperity, our scientific achievements, our position among the nations, our large-heartedness toward others in need—all these are praiseworthy.

Disappearance of Patriotism

But I am concerned about the disappearance of patriotism as a virtue. It is popular now to scoff at our nation's genesis, sneer at the great American traditions, and speak scathingly of the "American way of life" as though it were something unworthy or even wrong. I think that's a pity, really.

Every country has its faults. All you have to do is travel a little and you find that out.

Several years ago I was with a group that had ministered in the Orient and were now in Shanghai on the way home. Bone-tired and shivering, we climbed the several flights of stairs in an unheated building to get to the designated customs area where some 18 officials at separate desks peered at our documents and eventually stamped them. It was an agonizingly slow process.

Daws Trotman was just in front of me in the long line. Though a giant in most spiritual matters he was not noted for extreme patience. He got fed up with the delays.

Just as we arrived at what was the last desk he asked the official who faced us, "Can't you hurry this up a little?"

The man looked steadily at him and replied, "You are making this most difficult. Better you come back tomorrow." He turned and went away.

So we had to start all over again the next day.

Yes, every country—including our own—has its faults and foibles and red tape. The Latins have a word for this stalling process. They call it *papeleo*. The Spanish word for paper is *papel* and anything that involves paper shuffling (we call it red tape) the Latins call *papeleo*. There's lots of it around the world!

No, America is not perfect. But we are still, it seems to me, the greatest country in the world. Why do I say that? Because there is a residue here—a remnant of considerable size and influence—of people who worship Almighty God, who desire to do his will, and who seek to spread his gospel. What is more, the Spirit of God is blessing their lives and their efforts. They are imbued with the spirit of true patriotism.

According to Webster, patriotism is a love of country, a devotion to the welfare of one's country and a passion inspiring one to serve his country. One who holds this stance is a patriot. It bothers me that this kind of person seems to be becoming extinct in our society.

My father was a patriot. Always proud of his service in the Spanish American War, he lived with me and my family for a number of years before he had to be moved to a Veterans' Hospital where complete and continual care could be given to him. One day while he was with us he went out and bought a large American flag. His eyes were dimming; glaucoma had robbed him of most of his sight.

He handed me his prized purchase with a sharp military order, "Put up the flag, Boy, it's Memorial Day."

When the Stars and Stripes were fluttering from a flagpole in front of our Chicago home, my father went out on the sidewalk, snapped to attention, looked up long and lovingly through those dimming eyes and then turned to me and said, "It's your flag, Boy, and your country. Do your best for both of them."

My father loved his country with a holy passion. He fought for it. He magnified its good points. I say we need more men and women like him in this area. It shocks me to see that we don't have too many of his caliber.

Rise of Materialism

I'm concerned, too, over the rise of materialism as a substitute religion. People believe in things now instead of God.

Materialism is the ethical doctrine that consideration of material well-being, especially of the individual himself, should rule in the determination of one's conduct. Instead of that ancient biblical truth, "Righteousness exalteth a nation, but sin is a reproach to any people," we now say in effect, "Affluence exalteth a nation, but poverty is a reproach to any people."

Did you read Sam Levenson's book *Everything But Money*? It's a story of his own colorful boyhood. His parents were poor, but they helped their children grow up to be normal, well-adjusted adults, some of them attaining outstanding professional recognition. In the process, the children didn't even *know* they were poor!

Conversely, we are now inclined to say of any of life's values, if you can't quantify it, or analyze it, or package it, or sell it, or make a dollar on it—throw it out. Thus, because no one has yet been able to quantify God, or faith, or love, or loyalty, or righteousness (you can't package any of these or weigh out a pound of them) those concepts are being shelved in favor of acquired skills, material comforts, a shorter work week, personal indulgence, and so on.

We now have what is called the "new leisure." Millions of people have more time on their hands than they ever had before, and they consider that a "problem." Possessed of this "new leisure," many are bored stiff with life. They constantly seek something to relieve the unmitigated ennui they feel. Why? Because they have tossed out what makes life worth living.

Our Lord Jesus said in Luke 12: "A man's life consisteth

not in the abundance of the things which he possesseth"
(v. 15). To illumine his point he gave a parable about a rich
man. This man . . .

> . . . thought within himself . . . What shall I
> do, because I have no room where to bestow
> my fruits? . . . This will I do: I will pull down
> my barns and build greater . . . And I will say
> to my soul, Soul, thou hast much goods laid
> up for many years; take thine ease, eat, drink,
> and be merry. *But God said* unto him, Thou
> fool, this night thy soul shall be required of
> thee: then whose shall those things be, which
> thou hast provided? (Luke 12:16-20).

This yearning for "things" besets all of us. Bargain
prices, easy credit, the necessity to "keep up with the
Joneses"—all are inclined to blind us to matters of eternal
worth. I am startled and saddened when I see so many
Christians driving hard to increase their material possessions hoping to make these a substitute for faith in God. It
never works.

Weakening of National Value System
The third thing that bothers me is the weakening of our
national value system—a system which has always been
based on Judeo-Christian morality and the Bible.

Now we have the so-called new morality, situational
ethics that says: "just do what seems right at the time." Our
nation is floundering because we have lost the sense of any
absolutes. We have cast aside values which the Founding
Fathers held dear. Obviously, not every man who signed the
Declaration of Independence was a believer in Christ, as we
use that term. Some were deists and a few were honest
agnostics—at least one or two. But all of them had been
influenced by the Bible. Jefferson's language in that Declaration has the lofty quality of biblical prose. The concepts he
expressed were not derived primarily from any of the

philosophers or writers of his day. They were found, initially and always, in the Word of God.

But we have torn the Bible out of the fabric of our national life, with the result that the woof and the warp of it are disintegrating. Oh, we still induct our high officials by placing their hands on the Bible. We open the meetings of Congress with a prayer. We retain the words "In God We Trust" on our coins. We continue to have chaplains in the military forces of our nation, and I pray God that they may always be there. But in profound and far-reaching ways we have ruled God out and have weakened our whole value system.

I was in the courtroom on the day the Supreme Court heard the argument as to whether or not portions of the Bible should be permitted to be read at the beginning of a school day. The Court said no. In the decade that followed I saw the spread of pornography and the fearful rise in crime. While these conditions are attributable to more than one cause, of course, I cannot avoid the feeling that America is paying a tremendous price for tossing the Word of God and prayer out of the schoolroom.

I invite you to take inventory of your own personal values. For what would you be willing to be shot to death? I tell my students, "Find out what you are willing to die for and you will have a pretty clear idea of what you live for."

America has had a great history. Many of my readers have not only been recognized for great achievements themselves, but also have had illustrious and dedicated parents and grandparents. But righteousness is never inherited. Without embracing Tom Paine's philosophical system, I can agree with him heartily when he says, "In planning for posterity, we ought to remember that virtue is not hereditary." Each person must face his spiritual needs and their fulfillment by himself, with his God. The decision is personal, the challenge is to individual commitment to Jesus Christ: will I make it or will I not?

God Blesses

God blesses any people who seek and worship him. The Psalmist said, "Blessed (happy, fortunate) is the nation whose God is the Lord" (Psalm 33:12).

Whatever else may be said about our Founding Fathers, it is without question that they were, for the most part, God-fearing men. The writings of those early patriots abound in references to faith in God and one's duty to do his will.

Lincoln, in his farewell address at Springfield, Illinois, on February 11, 1861, said:

> I now leave not knowing when or whether I
> may return, with a task before me greater
> than that which rested upon Washington.
> Without the assistance of that Divine Being,
> who ever attended him, I cannot succeed.
> With that assistance, I cannot fail. Trusting in
> him who can go with me, and remain with
> you, and be everywhere for good, let us con-
> fidently hope that all will yet be well.

There you have it—the spirit of Lincoln and many others like him, whose faith in God was real and far-reaching.

And what has been the result of the demonstration of such faith? Even if one does not accept this cause-and-effect approach to the matter, it must be admitted that the United States of America, as a nation, has been blessed and prospered as few other nations have.

God gave Solomon the formula for receiving divine blessing:

> If my people, which are called by my name,
> shall humble themselves, and pray, and seek
> my face, and turn from their wicked ways;
> then will I hear from heaven, and will forgive
> their sin, and will heal their land (2 Chronicles
> 7:14).

Economic recovery, social improvement and military victory have often been tied to a revival of faith in God. As you read history books and the Bible together you will see that this is startlingly true.

God Judges

But God judges a people who turn away from him. "The wicked shall be turned into hell, and all nations that forget God" (Psalm 9:17).

The problem with America today is not so much that she is *against* God; she has simply *forgotten* him, ruled him out of her national life. We are, of course, not the only country that has done this.

I visited a certain country in Europe some years ago and commented on the fact that it was difficult to get a crowd in church on Sunday.

My listener replied rather sadly, "Oh, you don't understand, Mr. Cook. Sunday is the day for us to go to the mountains, to ski, to have fun. It is the day for young people and grownups alike to go in for sports of all kinds. Sunday is a bad day to get anybody to think about God."

Well, that's too bad, isn't it? The "forgetting" of God signs the death warrant of any nation. God always means what he says.

Blessing was promised to our first parents in the Garden of Eden.

> God blessed them, and God said unto them,
> Be fruitful and multiply, and replenish the
> earth (Genesis 1:28).

But punishment was to be meted out for disobedience:

> Of the fruit of the tree which is in the midst of
> the garden, God hath said, Ye shall not eat of
> it, neither shall ye touch it, *lest ye die* (Genesis
> 3:3).

Because God must always be true to his word, the sin-

ning pair suffered "death" the moment they disobeyed—
spiritual death first, and physical death later on, for them
and for the whole human race.

Trace the history of the children of Israel. With consum-
mate patience God warned them again and again. But ultimately, when there was no repentance or turning to him, the
blow fell.

We ought to pray that God will awaken us and in his
grace turn us back to him.

God Demands Choices
God prospers a people who choose to build on the Word of God.

In a well-known parable, Jesus pictured two men: one
wise and one foolish (Matthew 7:24-27). Both were builders.
Both made choices related to their work. The wise man
constructed his house on bed rock, and it easily withstood
the storms that assailed it. The foolish man built upon the
sand.

> And the rain descended, and the floods
> came, and the winds blew, and beat upon
> that house; and it fell: and great was the fall of
> it.

Why did the wise man have no fear? His house was built
on a strong foundation that he himself had selected. "These
sayings of mine," said Jesus, "are that foundation."

Our country, in its beginning, gave high priority to the
Word of God and worship. The foundation was firm. With
the years, we have made other choices, perhaps imprecepti-
bly—choices of self-seeking and forgetfulness of God—so
that our once strong foundation has begun to crumble.

It is high time for repair. It is time for return to the Word of
God and its authority over the individual and over the
nation.

God Works through a Personal Relationship
There is no substitute for a personal relationship with God.

It is possible to be a Christian in name, that is, officially a

member of any one of many denominations or interdenominational groups, without personal and total commitment to
Jesus Christ. But it is only commitment that brings satisfaction and power for service.

The problems of this life are spiritual, not primarily
economic, or sociological, or military. Only God has the
answers. And he gives them to those who will listen to
him—those who have *earned the right* to listen and to learn
because of their personal acceptance of the Lord Jesus
Christ.

God Comes in the Person of Christ

*The way to a personal relationship with God is through a
Person, the Lord Jesus Christ.*

We give over the complete control of our lives to that
blessed Person. This is something that you, and only you,
can do for yourself, and I for myself. Too often, we are not
ready to accept him.

An acquaintance of mine had a bad trip with drugs. She
was in a hospital with a felony charge against her. She had
stabbed a policeman in the course of a violent reaction to the
drugs she had taken.

I spoke to her. Was she happy about the way things were
going?

"No."

Would she like things to go differently in her life?

"Oh, yes."

Did she know about Jesus?

"Yes."

Did she know what she must do if she wanted to *know*
him?

"Yes."

What should she do?

"Accept him as Saviour."

Did she know what that meant, really?

"No."

So I took a few moments to explain that to accept Christ

as Saviour meant to let him come into your life and to give him complete control ot it. I said it means to let him make all the decisions that concern you, let him give the orders, let him run your life. Was she ready for that?

She thought for a long moment and then replied, very quietly, "All I can say, Mr. Cook, is that I'd have to think about that for a long time. I'm not ready for that yet."

You see, the trouble with many of us is that we are not *willing* to let God take charge of our lives.

Is he speaking to you at this moment? Do you feel, down deep in your heart, "Oh, I need to give myself to God?" If that is your reaction, receive him! You'll find from that moment on you will enjoy a personal relationship with the Lord that makes life—every moment of it—an adventure with him.

God Uses Men

The history of our great country is the story of the action and interaction of men. We look upon many of them as "great."

But did you know this: God will use *every* individual if only that individual will allow him to.

Think of the great heroes of faith pictured for us in the Bible. They were ordinary humans who had their faults, just as we do. They were made great, not by human effort, but by God's transforming grace.

Moses stammered and had a short temper.

Gideon was scared stiff, apparently afraid of his own shadow. We see him threshing grain in a wine press. (Try that sometime and see how hard it is!) Invading armies were all around that area, and should any tell-tale cloud of chaff rise into the morning air, it would be only minutes before soldiers would arrive to take away the grain and perhaps the thresher as well.

David was Israel's sweet singer, a good man with a slingshot and a great soldier. But he also had an eye for a beautiful woman—and this once became his downfall.

Daniel was a slave. He could boast no royal background, but he became prime minister under three dynasties.

James and John, who later became apostles, were men with a very short fuse; Christ called them "sons of thunder." They were not above conniving a little to get a better place in the kingdom they expected would be set up.

Whenever these names are mentioned, we scarcely think at all of the frailties and mistakes of the men they represent, but rather of how God used them. The greatest thing that could ever happen to you will occur when you bow in acknowledgment of the lordship of Jesus Christ in your life. He will make something of *you*, that you could never be without him.

Stuart Hamblen, well-known radio personality, tells of the time when he was brought to faith in Jesus Christ. A great evangelistic campaign was being led by Billy Graham in Los Angeles. Through his believing wife, Hamblen knew about these meetings and shied away from them. He ran off on a hunting trip to Utah. But a sudden snow storm forced him out of the mountains and he returned to Los Angeles, feeling sure he had stayed away long enough to have avoided any confrontation with the gospel. The meetings were scheduled to close that weekend.

He got home late on Sunday night and was greeted at the door by his wife, beaming. "Good news," she said, "they've extended the meetings one more week."

Well, Hamblen wasn't too happy about that; he went to bed, exhausted from his travels and his hunting. But he couldn't sleep. Finally the conviction of God was so strong upon him that he got up and said to his wife in his rough way, "Get dressed, woman. We're going to see Billy Graham."

So they started out, traveling across the city to the place where Mr. Graham and his song leader, Cliff Barrows, were staying, and woke them up.

Stuart Hamblen begged, "Billy, pray for me."

Billy Graham replied, "I'm not going to pray for you. I won't let you lie to me or to my God. You've got to get things right in your life before anybody can pray for you, or before you can even pray for yourself."

I heard Stuart Hamblen telling about this. He said, "I got down on my knees and I gave God my horse-racing, I gave him my filthy stories, I gave him my gambling, I gave him everything I could think of that was wrong in my life—and then I really began to pray."

As he tells this story he will smile and say, "Friends, then I heard the heavenly switchboard click in the skies"—his way of saying that he got through to God and God got through to him. Since that day, God has used the life and testimony of Stuart Hamblen in a remarkable way. God "made" him when he came to him in earnestness and sincerity.

The Future Brings Hope

But this happy condition will not just "happen."

We need to face honestly our laxness, our self-righteousness, our greed for possessions and power, our ignoring or forsaking of God and his clearly revealed will.

We need to experience contrition . . . confession . . . forgiveness . . . inner peace.

We need to embrace anew the divine principles laid down in God's Word.

In other words, *we* must do something. Then God, faithful to his promises, will come to our aid and gloriously help us. Remember:

> If my people which are called by my name,
> shall humble themselves, and pray, and seek
> my face, and turn from their wicked ways:
> *then* will I hear from heaven, and will forgive
> their sin, and *heal their land* (2 Chronicles 7:14).

20. Get at It!

Procrastinate: to put off from day to day; to defer; postpone.

Which of us has not at some time said, "I have to get at that job . . . tomorrow?" The tendency to put things off is as human as the tendency to want other things right away. It is an expression of basic, fallen, human nature.

Here are some of the causes of procrastination:

1. *Misplaced priorities.* We often give attention to the trivial while missing the eternal. A man remarked one day to the king of Israel, "As thy servant was busy here and there . . . he was gone!" The man he had been assigned to guard, he said, had slipped away while he was busy with other things. What other things? What can be as important as the task of guarding an important life? (1 Kings 20:40).

2. *Self-interest.* The wise man cautions, "Say not unto thy neighbor, Go, and come again, and tomorrow I will give; when thou hast it by thee" (Proverbs 3:28). The Pennsylvania Dutch have a saying which, loosely translated, says, "First me, then me, after that you, but not for a long time."

3. *Mistaken idea of your right to the future.* We often put off important actions or decisions on the assumption that tomorrow . . . there is always tomorrow, and one can do it then. Not so. "Boast not thyself of tomorrow; for thou knowest not what a day may bring forth," Solomon cautioned. And James, the Apostle of directness, says, "Your life is a vapor. Ye ought to say, If the Lord will, we shall live, and do this, or that." Felix, too, gambled on the uncertain future. "Go thy way for this time," he said. "When I have a convenient season, I will call for thee."

4. *Mistaken assumptions.* The antediluvians assumed that

it would not rain, and waited too long to heed Noah's preaching. One imagines there were plenty of seekers after salvation when it was too late. Members of Lot's family assumed that there was plenty of time to get out of Sodom, until the fire of God fell. Mary and Joseph assumed that there was plenty of time to look for the boy Jesus at the end of one day's journey. "They, supposing him to have been in the company, went a day's journey; and (then) they sought him among their kinsfolk and acquaintances."

Here are some things you can do to lick the tendency to put things off:

1. *Recognize procrastination as a sin, and repent of it.* "Therefore, to him that knoweth to do good, and doeth it not, to him it is sin," says James. Pray specifically and in faith for deliverance from your tendency to put things off. Christ is a great enough Saviour to save you from other sins. Is he not able for this one also? Colossians 2:6 indicates that just as you trusted him to save you, even so you can trust him step by step in your Christian life.

2. *Spend enough time with your Lord to get a clear sense of his direction.* He knows what is important, what is urgent, what must be attended to now. You will save yourself endless wasted hours and steps if you invest just a little more time in waiting "at headquarters" until you get your marching orders for the day.

3. *List the things that need to be done, and prioritize the list.* That means, place the most important item at the top of the list, the next most important item second on the list, and so on.

4. *Start with the first, most important, item on your list.* You will find often that it is also the most difficult. No matter . . . get at it! You will gain an immense sense of satisfaction at having finished the most important task for the whole day! Small thought here: If you can't "get started," say to yourself, "If I *were* going to start on this, what would I say or do?" Then follow through on those ideas, and presto, you *are* started.

5. *A performance aid: Set deadlines for yourself,* and make a

challenge of bettering your own times for any given task. "I am going to finish this book by nine-thirty," you may say to yourself. Your reading speed will automatically increase, and you will find yourself doing less daydreaming between paragraphs. To the complaint, "But then I wouldn't enjoy it," we simply have to say, "*Which* enjoyment do you wish— that of dawdling and dreaming, or the enjoyment of accomplishment?"

6. *Reset your priorities every day*—better still, the night before. There is a great advantage to be gained in planning the next day's work at the close of the day. For one thing, your accomplishments and failures are fresh in your mind, and you can learn from them and profit by them. For another thing, by planning the next day's work the night before, you give your unconscious mind a chance to work on the ideas all night while you sleep. Don't laugh! As I've already stated, you have a computer between your ears, and it never sleeps. Why not have it working for you, analyzing and solving tomorrow's problems while your body is resting?

7. *Make a habit of conscious dependence on the Holy Spirit.* Pray your way through every job, and through every day. This procedure will enlist the power of the Almighty in your work, and will save you endless hours of retracing your steps because of having gone down a dead-end street. Child of God, you have a right to the guidance of your Father! "The Lord shall guide thee continually," says Isaiah. And our Saviour promised that the Holy Spirit would "guide you into all truth." Paul declares that the sons of God are led by the Spirit of God. And James reminds us that if we lack wisdom, all we need do is ask of God, "who giveth to all men liberally, and upbraideth not." And Proverbs 3:5-6 reminds us that if you want the will of God, and ask for it, that is what you'll get: "He *shall* direct by paths."

8. *Make a life-time habit of immediate obedience* to what you know to be God's will at any given moment. Too often, what we call procrastination is just plain disobedience. Wait upon God until you know his will. Place the most important element of that will at the top of your list and then get at it!

21. What's Wrong with Work?

The way it looks from here, you'd think the great American dream is to get paid for doing nothing. We want a shorter work-week, with higher pay, so we'll have more time off to do nothing.

Of course, how it really works out is that we get our shorter hours, and we get our higher pay, and we also get a higher-priced set of needs and wants. Therefore we take a second job in our time off to pay for the obligations we assumed when we got our time off. It doesn't add up, does it?

To begin with, *God instituted work as the way human nature functions best.* "Six days shalt thou labor and do all thy work," God said in the ten commandments. Work for six days, rest and worship for one—that is God's schedule for us.

Work is part of the nature of God. "On the seventh day God ended his work which he had made; and he rested on the seventh day from all his work which he had made." "My Father worketh hitherto, and I work," said our Lord Jesus Christ. "I must work the works of him that sent me."

Work is God's plan for the Christian. "We are his workmanship, created in Christ Jesus unto good works, which God hath before ordained that we should walk in them." "Work out your own salvation with fear and trembling, for it is God which worketh in you, both to will and to do of his good pleasure." "This we commanded you, that if any would not work, neither should he eat . . . We exhort that with quietness they work, and eat their own bread."

Work is the stuff of which a successful testimony is made. "Let your light so shine before men, that they may see your good works, and glorify your Father which is in heaven." "Having

212

your manner of life honest among the Gentiles: that, where-as they speak against you as evildoers, they may by your good works, which they shall behold, glorify God."

And for the heart grown cold toward Christ—what will bring back that first love? "Repent," he says, "and do the first works." Working for the Lord makes you love him more and more!

Yes, *work is all right. Especially when it is harnessed to eternity:* "Whether therefore ye eat, or drink, or whatsoever ye do, do all to the glory of God . . . While we look not at the things which are seen, but at the things which are not seen: for the things which are seen are temporal; but the things which are not seen are eternal . . . Wherefore we labor, that we may be accepted of him."

22. The Future Belongs to You

Leonardo da Vinci said, "In rivers, the water that you touch is the last of what has passed and the first of that which comes: so with time present."

It is important to stop thinking of the future as something apart, a separate concept, something that is yet to arrive in your experience. Today is yesterday bearing fruit; and tomorrow is already here, in embryo, in essence, in small beginnings.

The direction of your future course is generally revealed by the set of your sails today. In other words, your future is already packaged—in your body and mind, in forces and faculties, in appetites and attitudes. The use or abuse of these potentials will largely determine your tomorrows.

Everybody knows this. Not everyone knows how to apply it, however. Here are some thoughts that may prove helpful to you.

1. *Check your values.* Today's value-system will shape tomorrow's choices. How do you rate the word *duty*, for instance, as over against *dollar*? Or how does *popularity* compare with *prayer*? Can *faith* hold its own when compared with *fun*? or *food*?

For once in your life, be ruthlessly honest with yourself. Ask, and answer these questions: "What are my real values? What means the most to me? What do I really seek, and what do I truly enjoy?" When you have the completely honest answer to this inquiry, you will also have a highly accurate profile of yourself in years to come—unless God, or evil forces change you.

2. *Examine your habits.* Your mental and physical habits of today will set your thought and performance patterns for years to come. How do you treat your body? What are your

thoughts? What do you do, and what do you think about when you don't *have* to do anything? Do you know anything of physical and mental discipline? The answer to these questions will reveal clearly the direction in which your life is moving.

3. *List your skills.* Your skills development of today will largely shape the skills of tomorrow. Are you learning basic techniques that will be useful in our complex world? Typing? Shorthand? Bookkeeping? Engineering and electronics? Mechanical skills? Management and human engineering? Psychology, and how to get along with people? Take inventory of your skills, and realize that they are already beginning to limit your potential usefulness throughout a lifetime. If you have few skills, start acquiring some!

4. *Watch your reactions.* Your instinctive reactions, based on various "learned responses" to situations, will be projected into later life. If this frightens you, let it: Your peers, and your superiors, will rate you largely on your reactions while under stress. Better make sure you're reacting right. Do you lash out at people in impatience? Do you sulk when corrected? Do you quit when the going gets rough? Do you insist on your own way? Or do you consider pressure situations as challenges, and as problems to be solved by careful thought and prayer? Allow God to change your reactions in the direction of his Word and his will, so tomorrow's reactions will be better.

5. *Learn that life is "for keeps."* Nothing you do or say is ever lost. Everything counts. Everything is registered in your memory and unconscious mind. Each separate experience becomes a part of everything else in your life. You will always have to live with your memories, because they have become part of the real you. They are the stuff of which your present life is made up. Yes, life is "for keeps." You can never afford to say, "What I do now doesn't count." It always does.

Today's world will either give you a helping hand, or a kick, depending on your attitude, and how you measure up to the new standards of excellence.

A nurse, for instance, with her R.N. and a B.S. degree, can now obtain grants and scholarships that will take her all the way to an M.D. and specialization in the field of her choice.

The same thing holds true for people interested in the various branches of science and math. If you "have it," and are willing to work, you will receive lots of encouragement, and job offers aplenty.

On the other hand, if you are content merely to "get by," you will soon find out that automation can do very well without the unskilled laborer.

6. Last of all, learn early the lesson that the things which harm you, as well as those which build you up are spiritual in nature. Lust and pride, envy and jealousy, selfishness and laziness—all are maladies of the spiritual life, are they not? And clear-eyed faith which submits human ambition to the will of God and sanctifies human "drive" until it is one with the dynamics of the Holy Spirit—these also are matters that affect the human spirit before they ever show up in thought, word or deed. Well did Solomon say (Proverbs 4:23), "Keep thy heart with all diligence; for out of it are the issues of life."

Success in the future depends on a heart surrendered to Jesus Christ, today!

In this part of the book I have been talking about your own personal walk with the King. But some people over-emphasize personal piety and treat the members of their family in anything but a Christlike way. I now want to give you five ways to improve your home life. That's the hardest place of all to walk with the King.

PART THREE:
YOUR FAMILY WALK

23. Tell the Truth

Consider one way to improve your home life . . . *Tell the truth*.

You see, truth became your way of life when you trusted the Lord Jesus Christ. Now, if you haven't trusted Christ as Saviour, you can do it before you've finished reading this page. You can bow humbly and say "Lord, I know I'm a sinner and I know that Jesus died for sinners and I now repent of my sins and turn to Christ. I'll trust you as my Saviour." He'll save you from sin. This is what he says he will do. "If any man hear my voice, and open the door, I will come in to him and will sup with him, and he with me."

But if my readers are already saved, then you have to remind yourself that *when you trusted the Lord Jesus Christ as Saviour, truth became your way of life*.

Our Lord Jesus Christ is, himself, the truth. He said, "I am the way, the truth and the life. No man cometh unto the Father but by me."

We read in John 1:17, "Grace and truth came by Jesus Christ." Our Lord Jesus said to his disciples and thus to us as well, "Ye shall know the truth and the truth shall make you free."

So, living the truth . . . telling the truth . . . experiencing the truth . . . being a demonstration of God's truth . . . all of this became a way of life when you trusted Christ as Saviour.

John says in 1 John 3:19 "Hereby know we that we are of the truth."

You actually belong to a group that is marked or identified by truth as the very stuff of which life is made.

The ministry of the blessed Holy Spirit is to guide us into all truth (John 16:13). "He shall guide you into all truth."

Now you can see the difference between this way of life and that which is practiced by most of the rest of the world. In Communist countries, for instance, it is not thought at all necessary to tell the truth as we think of it. Anything that serves the purposes of the state, and anything that advances the cause of Communism . . . this is considered to be the right thing to do.

We, however, who follow the teachings of the Word of God and do trust Christ as Saviour, are different. We aren't content with casuistry. We aren't content with saying "Well, if it brings the right results, then it must be right for me."

No, a thousand times no! We will only be content with the truth. You will find that your home life improves when you specialize in living the truth, telling the truth, being a demonstration of God's truth all day long.

That leads me then to the second thought:

Decide that *there is* no possible *alternative* to *living the truth*.

John says in 1 John 1:6, "If we say we have fellowship with him and walk in darkness, we lie and do not the truth." He says further "No lie is of the truth" (1 John 2:21).

This is not only a matter of saying, then, but of doing.

You see, it is possible to act a lie as well as to tell a lie and it is possible to tell a lie while saying things that are accurate.

I suppose most of you have heard the old chestnut about the lady who, during World War II days was having difficulty in renting an apartment because she had a large family and children. So finally she hit upon an expedient that worked. She went to the rental agent and asked for a place and he said "Do you have any children?" She took out her handkerchief and, wiping her eyes, said, "All my children are in the cemetery." He rented the apartment to her and after she had signed the lease, she went out and over to the local cemetery and said "Come on, kids." They got in the car and went over to the house. They were in the cemetery all right, but she had told a big whopping lie, hadn't she?

Well, you have to decide on this. I think many people

have an attitude like that of the little boy when he misquoted a couple of verses by putting half and half together. It came out this way: "A lie is an abomination to the Lord and a very present help in time of trouble."

I think many of us feel that way. We say, "Well, I want to tell the truth but there are times when you just can't. I want to live true to God but there are some times when you just have to compromise."

You have to decide this for yourself. I can't decide it for you. You have to make up your mind . . . there's no alternative to the truth.

Now we come to the third point: *Put truth into your daily relationships.*

I suppose all of us under oath would be pretty accurate but sometimes we are highly inaccurate in daily relationships.

Paul says, "Henceforth, be no more children tossed to and fro and carried about with every wind of doctrine but, speaking the truth in love, grow up into him in all things, even unto Christ."

Speaking the truth in love. Put truth, bathed in Calvary love, into all of your daily relationships.

Now, in every home, there are certain touchy situations that arise from time to time and they relate to all sorts of things—in-laws, money, school, who can have the car, etc.

As a matter of fact, a lot of touchy situations arise out of normal living. We don't look for them. We don't set out on any given day to have an argument . . . it's just part of living, this certain amount of gravel that you have to face.

Now, how are you going to face it? Well, you can run away from it. You can evade it. You can detour carefully around it, or you can face it honestly.

The finest thing in the world is to be honest about situations that are a little bit edgy and gravelly and touchy.

Why don't you try that? Instead of getting all upset with each other, just face the thing frankly, whatever it is, and say "Let's talk about this and see what's what." It won't hurt a bit and you'll find when you get into the habit of facing up to things immediately, life becomes a good deal more calm and easy and enjoyable.

It's a mark of immaturity to blow up and run away. You know this. My father used to say that you can swear just as effectively by slamming a door as you can by saying the words because everybody knows what you mean.

So, it's a mark of being a little boy or a little girl when you refuse to face up to things frankly and instead, you blow your top and lose your temper and back off and slam the door and kick the dog and sulk. This is a great gambit, you know. The silent treatment . . . just go and sulk for six weeks and by and by everybody just goes quietly crazy trying to cope with you.

It's a lot easier just to face things, isn't it? Put truth into your daily relationships.

Another thing, let's learn to admit our failings readily.

How long has it been since you said to anybody, "You know the trouble with me is I am so sensitive that I am always defending myself." Or, "The trouble with me is I'm proud." Or, "The trouble with me is I'm lazy." Or, "The trouble with me is I'm jealous."

Have you ever admitted anything to anybody?

You see, the Bible says, "Confess your faults one to another, and pray one for another that ye may be healed."

You'd be surprised how much strain goes out of daily living if you are just willing to admit your failings quickly.

I read somewhere a whimsical article that purported to give advice to husbands. It said "When everything else fails and you have done something there is no good excuse for, just look her right in the eye and say, 'That was terribly stupid of me, wasn't it?'" Well, you might try that. It might work. Just to admit our failings to each other . . . just to say, "Well, that's how it is. I admit it. I did it, or I said it, etc." might save a situation many times.

Then, never trim the truth to save your own skin.

The compromiser lives to be run over by his own compromise. The liar lives to be caught in his own web of deceit and the advantage that you think you are going to get never arrives. You never get any real advantage out of trimming the truth. And the price you pay is a tremendous price.

Did you know that you have to remember all the lies you tell so you don't get caught up in your own lie?

I used to tell the fellows in Youth for Christ, "Always tell the truth, then you don't have to try to remember what you said last."

Never trim the truth to save your own skin.

And finally always tell the truth in love."

Paul says in Ephesians 4: "Speaking the truth in love."

I'll tell you, the way you say a thing makes a lot of difference, doesn't it?

You know the old wheeze about saying, "When I look at you I lose all sense of the passage of time." Another way to say it is, "Your face would stop a clock." That's not so good, is it? Well, speak the truth in love.

Let the love of God be real in your heart and let it show in your voice when you speak to people.

Always tell the truth in love.

Tell the truth today.

24. Fall in Love All Over Again

Today, *fall in love all over again.*

You're familiar, of course, with Ephesians 5:25, "Husbands, love your wives." Now, this is not a matter of option. It's not a matter of whether or not you ever get around to it or whether you feel like it. As a matter of fact, sometimes you don't feel very much like it, do you?

Well, it says "Husbands, love your wives, even as Christ also loved the Church and gave himself for it."

The relationship of husband and wife in a Christian home is precisely that of the Lord Jesus Christ to his Church.

I think it would be a good idea for us to realize, in this day of wobbly marriages and disintegrating homes and splitting up couples, that *God's way is to stay in love for keeps.*

There are certain ways you can do this, you know. We'll get at them a little later. But let's start off by reminding ourselves that God intends a man to stay in love with his wife and God intends a woman to stay in love with her husband. The years may pass and they may get to be the victims of the 6-Bs. You know what the 6-Bs are? Baldness, Bifocals, Bridgework, Bulges, Bunions and Bicarbonate. Yes, the years may pass and you may get to be the victim of the aging process but you can be very much in love.

This is the basis, really, this Christian love—this openhearted commitment to each other . . . each to the other and both to God; this is the basis of a happy Christian life together.

Husbands, love your wives. Wives, love your husbands.

The real question with many a person is "Have I drifted away?" "Has my heart grown cold?" "Have I forgotten to do or say the things that keep love alive?"

And then a second step about this matter of love in the Christian home is to realize that *love is the basic atmosphere of the Christian life*. Romans 5:5 says "The love of God is shed abroad in our hearts by the Holy Ghost which is given unto us."

And we read in Ephesians 3:17 that a Christian is to be ". . . rooted and grounded in love."

Rooted and grounded in love.

The very what-ness of our life together is the love of God. This is what it is all about.

Paul, writing to Titus, said that before a person gets to know the Lord Jesus, he is hateful and he hates other people. "We were hateful," he says, "and hating one another." We were filled with resentment and hatred. This is the way it is in the jungle of the world, among those who are godless and without hope: "Hate-filled and hating one another." As a Christian, if you open your heart to the Lord Jesus and let him come in, the Holy Spirit of God fills your life with love. This is the very atmosphere of your life in a Christian home.

Now, sometimes it doesn't sound very much like it, does it? That's why we need to take a second look at the way we are living. We need to ask ourselves, "Has the atmosphere of my home been one of love, or resentment and argument and bickering and senseless anger and recriminative actions that were taken just to make the other person feel bad? Just tell yourself the truth about this. If there's room for improvement—(someone has said that the biggest room in any house is the room for improvement)—well, if there's room for improvement in your performance there, let's get started with an atmosphere of real love.

And love is not only in the saying but in the doing, isn't it? "Be ye kind one to another, tender-hearted, forgiving one another as God for Christ's sake has forgiven you. And walk in love as dear children."

This is the advice that God gives us: Live in love.

And how can you live in love?

Be kind. Be tender-hearted. Be forgiving . . . just as God has forgiven you and me our sins.

Well, that's a pretty big order, isn't it?

How does this all come about?

When the Holy Spirit of God is in one's life, love gets a chance to show what it can do. I am looking now at 1 Corinthians . . . "Love suffereth long and is kind. Love envieth not, love vaunteth not itself, is not puffed up . . . does not behave itself unseemly . . . seeketh not her own . . . is not easily provoked . . . thinketh no evil . . . rejoices not in iniquity but rejoices in the truth . . . beareth all things, believeth all things, hopeth all things, endureth all things. Love never faileth."

The very atmosphere of your life is the love of God in every day's relationships.

Now, how does this work out? Well, there's a verse in Galatians 5 that says, don't use your Christian liberty as an occasion to your old fleshly, sinful nature but in Galatians 5:13, it says "By love serve one another." .

Later on we are going to talk about a Christian home as a base for service but for now, let's remind each other that love never has the gimmies. It doesn't just grab for itself. It sees what it can do to help the other person . . . how much it can serve.

Real Christian love says "How may I help? How may I serve? How may I be of service? How may I have a ministry? How may I edify and build up? How may I encourage?" By love, serve one another.

Now, let's make this very practical.

Some days you've had some rough weather in your home and you say "Well, it's not my fault. I'd be willing to get along but the other person won't get along."

Well, maybe that's true. I'm not prepared to say that it isn't. But why not ask this question: Now, how can I be of service to this person that I've been having difficulty getting along with? How can I be of service? How can I really help?

Dr. Walter Wilson gave this advice to a young Christian

one time who was trying to win her unsaved father-in-law to Christ. He told her "Just make the dish he likes the most to eat and bring it to him and say 'Grandpa, I love you.' And you keep on, and you'll win him with your love."

The first time she did that, he batted the dish out of her hand and the hot liquid scalded her. She came back to Dr. Wilson's meeting with a bandage on her arm and said "It didn't work." He said "You keep on." Soon she was back with a smile and said, "It worked. One day I heard the sound of his wheel chair coming across the kitchen floor and I turned around. There he was, with a big tear running down his face and he said, "Oh Mary, will you pray for a wicked old man?"

You see, love did it. By love serve one another.

If you want to improve your home life, fall in love and make love the basis of service to others.

"Beloved," he said, "let us love one another. If God so loved us, we *ought* also to love one another." This is not a matter of option. Someone said, "I don't see how I can love some people, they are unloveable." Say, did you take a look at yourself before Calvary? What did God see in you that was any good that he should bestow his love upon you? "Herein is love, not that we loved God, but that he loved us and sent his Son to be the propitiation for our sins."

So it is not a matter of whether the other person is lovable, it is whether or not you are willing to obey God. He told us we should do it.

Here's another thing, and I am bringing in this truth more or less by implication but it is true. We read in 1 John 4:18 that "Perfect love casteth out fear." Do you know that often we get on the wrong side of people and we have trouble getting along with them simply through fear and resentment? We are a little afraid of them and we resent them and as a result, we get in trouble with them. Isn't that true?

Now, he says, "Perfect love casteth out fear." Where there is real love, there isn't any fear. You'll notice this. When you come to the place where your heart is absolutely open to another person, well, you won't have any difficulty getting along with him. He'll still have the same number of faults but somehow, that real love will have covered a great deal of the areas of abrasion and irritation.

Perfect love.

When you exercise the love of God in your home, you get along better in everyday situations.

Over in Revelation 2:4, 5, our Lord Jesus Christ mentions the fact that the Church at Ephesus had left its first love for Christ. And he says, "Repent therefore, and do the first works, or else I will come unto thee quickly and will remove thy candlestick...."

"Repent and do the first works."

You've left your first love. Your heart has grown cold, said he, toward your Saviour. Now, repent and do the first works—the things you did when first you fell in love with Jesus.

What does this mean so far as our home life is concerned?

Do you remember when you first fell in love? There wasn't anything you weren't willing to do for the object of your affection. You'd go out of your way to see him or her. You would do anything to please that individual. Some of you have gotten so far away from it you've forgotten. It's a good thing to remind ourselves, isn't it?

You would bring flowers ... candy ... do nice little things. If your boy friend was coming, you'd bake him a pie or something. Remember that? You did some things that showed your love and interestingly enough the more you did, the more you loved him, isn't that right? The more you did for that person, the more you loved him because when love gets in action, it grows as the basis of that action.

"Repent and do the first works."

What are the first works?

Nice little things that you do for people that you love. How effective it is. Try it for yourself today. Try doing something special without any reason for it. Don't say anything about it. Don't make a big fuss about it. Don't announce it with a trumpet blast, just do something nice without any special reason for it, just because you love the other person and say so. You'll be surprised what it will do to your home life. These little extra touches of love without any reason for it, you know. It isn't just climbing up on somebody's lap and saying "Dear daddy, I love you, give me a dollar." That isn't the psychology we're after here at all. You know that. It's just that little extra something that comes from a heart of love.

And then our Lord Jesus said to Simon Peter, "Do you love me? Do you really love me?" And after he had asked him three times, Simon Peter broke down and said, "Lord, thou knowest all things. Thou knowest that I love thee."

Then Jesus said, "Feed my sheep . . . ."

The right relationship with people, oftentimes, comes from a right relationship with Jesus, and so I have to say this: Love is the atmosphere of a normal Christian home. If you want things to go better in your home, fall in love all over again but if you want to make the right start in that direction, open your heart all over again to Jesus Christ. That's what makes home sweetest of all, when the people within that home love the Lord Jesus with everything that's within them.

Fall in love and fall in love, most of all, with the Lord Jesus Christ. Where he is Lord, there is liberty and there is love.

25. Learn to Pray

Today, *learn to pray.*

First, *have your own quiet time.* Do you know what we mean when we say "Have a quiet time?" That's a time, generally at the beginning of the day, when you look into the Word of God and let God speak to you and when you pray and open your heart and in the process, of course, open up the whole day to God. A quiet time.

From Pastor Stephen Olford I received a formula that has served me well through these many years. Said he, "You ought to stay with some given portion of Scripture until it *says* something to you."

This must be more that just reading the Bible dully and routinely. Read and meditate over a portioñ until it really speaks to your heart.

Second, write down what the Lord said to you through his Word. When the Scripture you are reading says something, write that down immediately in a note book of some sort.

Third, pray back to the Lord what he has said to you. Pray it back until your heart is warm and tender with the message.

Fourth, share it with someone as soon as you can. This is a good formula for feeding on the Word and having an effective quiet time.

I recently reread the story of John G. Paton, a great missionary. He spoke about his own boyhood home. He said, "Our home consisted of just three rooms; they called it the but and the ben and the mid-room or chamber, called the closet." Then he goes on to describe the one part of the humble oak cottage which was a combination kitchen and workshop and the other which was filled with beds and closets, etc.

"Then," he said, "this smaller middle room was a very small apartment betwixt the other two, having room only for a bed, a little table and a chair with a diminutive window showing diminutive light on the scene. This was the sanctuary of that cottage home.

"Thither daily and oftentimes each day, generally after each meal, we saw our father retire there and shut the door. And we children got to understand by a sort of spiritual instinct that the thing was too sacred to be talked about. The prayers were being poured out there for us as of old by the high priest within the veil in the most holy place. We occasionally heard the pathetic echoes of a trembling voice pleading as if for life and we learned to slip out and in past that door on tiptoe so as not to disturb the holy conversation. The outside world might not know but we knew whence came that happy light as of a new born smile that always was dawning on my father's face. It was a reflection," John G. Paton goes on to say "from the Divine Presence in which he lived."

He goes on to say "There were 11 of us brought up in a home like that, and in the resurrection every one of those children will rise up at the mention of their parents' names and call them blessed."

Isn't that beautiful? That's the way it ought to be. A person who learns how to walk with God by himself in a quiet time with the Lord will always have a greater influence in his home.

Have your own quiet time. Learn how to walk with God yourself. You'll find that it immediately improves your home condition.

Now, second, *maintain regular family worship.*

This is a custom that seems to be dying out in many places. We need to remind ourselves that one of the best ways to preserve a Christian home is to meet regularly around the Word of God.

Again, John G. Paton's father was faithful in the exercise

of family prayers. "He began," says Paton, "that blessed custom of family prayer morning and evening which my father practiced without one single omission until he lay on his death bed at 77 years of age, when even to the last of his life a portion of Scripture was read and his voice was heard softly joining in the Psalm and his lips breathed the morning and evening prayer, falling in sweet benediction on the heads of all his children, some far away, but all meeting him there at the Throne of Grace."

John G. Paton goes on to say, "None of us remember that any day ever passed unhallowed thus." "No hurry for market, no rush for business, no rival of friends or guests, no trouble or sorrow, no joy or excitement ever prevented our kneeling around the family altar while the high priest led our prayers to God and offered himself and children there. And blessed to others as well as to ourselves was the light of such example. I have heard that in long afteryears, the worst woman in the village who was then leading an immoral life, but since changed by the grace of God, was known to declare that the only thing that kept her from despair and from the hell of suicide when in the dark winter nights she crept close up underneath my father's window and heard him pleading in family worship that God would convert the sinner from the error of her wicked ways.

"She said she felt that she was a burden on that good man's heart and she knew God would not disappoint him. That thought kept her out of hell and at last led her to her Saviour."

Family prayers. Family worship. Time with the family to read the Bible and pray. It doesn't have to be long and it doesn't have to be boring. Ladies and gentlemen, family worship doesn't have to be boring. It can be interesting!

Read a portion of Scripture, not a long one. Comment upon it if you wish so that it can be understood and then lift an earnest prayer for the members of your family so that the presence of God becomes real, with your children, with your dear ones.

Find the time of day when most of you are likely to be

together. In many cases, it's after the evening meal. Bring the presence of your blessed Lord into your home.

If you want to improve your home life, maintain regular family worship.

Now in the next place, *use prayer as God's way of getting things done.*

Philippians 4:6-7 says—don't worry about anything. "Be careful for nothing" is the way it reads in the Authorized Version, "but in everything, by prayer and supplication, with thanksgiving, let your request be made known unto God, and the peace of God which passeth all understanding shall keep your hearts and minds through Christ Jesus."

Use prayer as God's divine leverage. You'd be surprised at the amount of spiritual vitamins that it will put into your family prayers if you will pray specifically about things. Let's not be content with just running drearily down the usual order, "Lord bless us and our relatives and the missionaries and the pastor, etc." Let's have a little more than that.

Get a prayer list of specific requests that you will be holding before the Lord in prayer and then, with your family, as well as in your own private praying, *be specific.* "When ye pray . . . say!"

Have something to say to God . . . not mumbling repetitions or striving to create some emotional effect but really transacting business with God.

Another thing—hang on to prayer until you get the answer.

It's not enough to just mention a request one day and forget it. God wants us to pray *until* the answer comes. It is time to seek the Lord—*until* he come and reign righteousness upon you.

The New Testament quotes our Lord Jesus as saying "Ask and keep on asking. Knock and keep on knocking. Seek and keep on seeking." And you will get an answer. You will receive. You will find the door will be open unto you.

There's a little song that goes "Just keep on praying 'til light breaks through" and this is mighty good advice.

Then when the Lord does answer prayer, praise the Lord

as a family. We were praying for the supply of a special need some years ago and God answered that prayer wonderfully with one single check. Well, you can know that it was a source of great joy when I brought the check with me to the supper table, laid it on the table and said, "Let's thank the Lord in answer to prayer."

So remember to praise the Lord, with your family, when he answers prayer.

Next, *learn to pray with individuals naturally and without strain*. Most folk recoil a little at the idea of praying with anybody unless it is at a time when you are supposed to be officially religious. That is to say, if you're in church, you feel it is the right thing to do, to pray, especially if somebody else does it. Or, if you're in trouble and want some help from the Lord right away, then you pray with a certain desperation of faith and feel all right about that. But when somebody is talking with you in a situation that is not necessarily religious, at a social gathering, in a store, on the street, driving in a car, wherever it may be, then sometimes we recoil a little at the idea of praying then because—well, we aren't used to it, frankly.

Let's learn to pray with individuals in nonreligious situations.

A good illustration of this is the life of a dear brother who was "promoted to glory," several years ago. Our brother, T. J. Bach, was one of the founders of the Evangelical Alliance Mission. He spent a good many years as a missionary in Venezuela and then came back to be the director of that mission for many more years. He was a precious, wonderful brother who brought the presence of God into many lives.

I am sure many of my readers remember T. J. Bach.

Well, do you remember also that whenever he met you, he hadn't been talking with you for more than 60 seconds until he had his hand on your shoulder and he was saying, "Now, dear brother, let's pray for you—" and he would really pray for you until you would feel the presence of God.

I recall meeting him in a bookstore in Chicago where I was trying to pick out some books. The conversation went something like this: "Dear brother Bach, how are you?" "Oh, I'm just fine, how are you?" We talked for just a few seconds and then he put his hand on my shoulder and silenced whatever I was saying and said, "Now, dear brother, we pray for you." And he prayed and God met us—right there in the middle of this bookstore!

I have prayed with T. J. Bach on the street and in committee meetings and in churches, and all over. He was just immediately in the presence of the Lord. What a precious memory he left behind him! He was a man who learned to pray with individuals, without any stress or strain.

This is what kept some of the G. I.s who were captured as prisoners during the Korean war and elsewhere during the brain-washing through which they were forced to go. Some of them cracked up because they didn't have any real, practical access to God. But there were others who could pray any moment, any time, and God was real and near.

One of the G. I.s said, "My God was as real to me as the back of my hand and as near." That's it! Let's learn to pray with people, in our homes, anywhere!

26. Make Your Home Definitely Christian

Make your home definitely Christian.

The first thing to do about this is to *make a decision that your home will be a Christian home.*

Many people have merely drifted into the kind of a home they have. They don't give much thought to it. They say "Well, we'd like a nice home. We'd always like to live well . . . carpets on the floors and drapes on the windows. Nice furniture and everything insured and enough money to make payments so the house will be ours by and by. We'd like to be happy in our home." This is all part of the way they feel about things. But really, they have never decided—husband and wife and the children who are old enough to have any share in what goes on, they've never decided what kind of a home it's going to be.

It might well be that you get together in a family council (that's a good thing to have anyway); you ought to get together and talk it over. Say, "Look, we've been sort of careless about the type of home we have. We like each other. We live well together but how about this—shouldn't we have a really Christian home?"

Now, what kind of a home would that be?

It would be characterized by Christian people, folk who really know the Lord Jesus as their Saviour, and Christian service.

Make your decision about this as a family. If you want to improve your home life, for once in your life, decide what kind of a home you want. And then go at it!

In the second place, let's *settle the matter of devotion.* A Christian home ought to have regular periods of devotion.

We call it "the family altar." Now, of course, there are all sorts of excuses about this. Everybody is too busy, or we all eat at different times so we are never together, etc.

Okay, if you want to major in excuses, go ahead. Anybody can give an alibi for his failures but if you'd really like to succeed in a Christian home, then give some thought to the matter of your family altar.

Did you know it only takes a few seconds, really, to read a Psalm and to offer an earnest prayer with your family? You're not that busy, are you? Are you so busy you couldn't spare God a minute or two?

And really, when you get into it, the family will enjoy this regular contact with the Lord.

Now, some of you say, "Well, we have small children and they don't understand."

Oh yes, they do understand! Very young children can understand that at a certain point in the day we bow our heads and we pray. And then, think of the joy that will be yours, When your youngster says, "Well, it's time to pray, now," and that little head goes down and hands are folded and you realize that early in life the habit of devotion has been established.

A really Christian home, a definitely Christian home, ought to have regular periods of devotion.

If you want a little more help in having family worship, you'll find a number of helpful books along this line in your Christian bookstore, but basically what's involved is reading a short passage of Scripture and then, perhaps, if the family likes to sing, singing a verse of a well-known hymn and praying.

Pray for the members of your family and your loved ones. Pray for your church and your pastor. Pray for your country and those who are in authority. Pray for yourself that God will make you the right kind of a person and a blessing to the rest of the family circle ... a real earnest, genuine prayer. Don't drift into formality here, now, because children can always tell whether or not it is real. An earnest, sincere and preferably brief prayer will do it.

Remember, neither prayers nor sermons have to be eternal to be immortal. A brief prayer will serve the purpose.

Do your long praying in private. Do your short praying in public.

In the next place, *a definitely Christian home ought to have Christian demeanor.* That's a long word meaning "act like a Christian."

I'm surprised at the number of homes where fighting and arguing seem to be the order of the day. Christian homes, I mean, where people talk back to each other and where they use rough and coarse and discourteous expressions to each other.

Of course, some of us were brought up differently. I had to be respectful to my father or I would have awakened on the other side of the room, I think. He believed in the Scriptural laying on of hands . . . the application of the board of education to the seat of knowledge, you know. So some of us were brought up a little differently.

But regardless of what your background may be, it makes sense,—doesn't it?—to look at each other in the family circle and say "Let's act like Christians. We don't have to shout at each other. We don't have to have fights and feuds and arguments. We can be polite to each other. There's no law that says we may not be nice to each other . . . simply because we live in the same family."

Christian demeanor in the home. Instead of shouting, you can speak in a well-modulated tone of voice. Instead of just piling into your food like a pig, you can use good table manners. Instead of using slang and coarse expressions, you can use language that marks you a lady or gentleman, and that honors and glorifies the Lord Jesus Christ. Christian demeanor. . . . Act like a Christian. . . . It's a very good idea.

Some of us forget this. We get so used to each other, home gets to be a place where we feel we can let down— where we don't have to be nice to anybody.

Always remember, there never is a moment when you may say to yourself, "Well, it doesn't matter now what I say."

It *always* matters! If you speak roughly or crudely or discourteously or without love, it leaves scar tissue in the hearts of those to whom you speak. So act, and talk and behave yourself as a Christian ought to.

"Whatsoever ye do in word or deed," Paul says, "do all in the name of the Lord Jesus, giving thanks unto God the Father by him."

And over in 1 Corinthians 10:31, "Whether therefore ye eat, or drink or whatsoever ye do, do all to the glory of God."

Christian demeanor. Act like a Christian.

Another thing that will make the home definitely Christian *is to make it distinctively Christian.* Let's get at this by reminding ourselves that to every child, as well as to parents there comes, sooner or later, the realization that a Christian home is different.

I think we'd better face this. It's not that we want to be different . . . it is that we *are* different, because we are Christians.

"If any man be in Christ, he is a new creation. Old things have passed away, behold all things are become new."

There *is* a difference and whether or not you want it so, it is so, when you receive the Lord Jesus Christ. *He makes the difference* in your life.

Now, the same thing is true of Christian homes. Don't wince at that difference but be proud of it. Of course, we're Christians and of course, our home is a Christian home and we're glad it is that way! Be glad that your home is different and capitalize on the difference.

Is your home quiet instead of filled with strife? Be glad about it and thank God that it is different.

Is your home a place of love and joy instead of a place filled with hatred and envy and jealousy? Thank God for the difference.

Is your home a place where, when some kind of junk

comes on the television you simply and quietly turn it off or turn to a different channel? Well, be glad there's a difference instead of alibing and excusing and being embarrassed about it. Stand a little taller, and hold your head high and say, "Yes, we are Christians. Yes, we do have a Christian home and thank God it's so!"

Make your home definitely—that is to say—distinctively Christian.

Let's see what we've said so far.

Make a decision that your home is going to be Christian.

Maintain regular devotions and a family altar.

Be careful to maintain Christian demeanor. Act like a Christian.

Capitalize on the distinction of having a Christian home.

Exercise determination that your home is not going to become a victim of materialism or secularism or compromise. Dare to stand against the tide!

Do you know that if you simply allow any building to stand by itself, without upkeep, it will fall down? The same thing is true of the Christian home. You do not drift into a happy home life. You have to work at it! So let's exercise determination to make the home happy and Christian. We are going to pray together. We are not going to let anything come between us and our God.

Someone says, "Well, I have to leave early, I can't stay for family worship."

Allright, once in a while this may be so. The schedule may be such that one or two members of the family may not be present at the time when you ordinarily pray. So then, get the rest of the family together anyway. Let's seek the Lord or let's pray earnestly for those who are absent at the time.

Then let's make opportunity to pray with those who missed out. If there's a chance to get with them later on . . . just whisper a prayer together to our blessed Lord.

The same thing is true of materialism.

"Why can't we have as many things as our neighbors?"

Or "Why can't we do this, that or the other things ?" "Why can't we take the family car and go for a picnic on Sunday? Of course, we'll miss church and of course, we'll miss Sunday school but why can't we do it like the others?"

You see, there's the subtle temptation to give in to yourself while neglecting Almighty God. Materialism and secularism. More time for self and more time for the world and less time for God. This is inevitably the trend of our day and you can, and must, stand against it in your home.

Gather the family together every so often and talk about this and say, "Look, let's be Christian . . . in our lives, and in our actions . . . and in our words and in our attitudes. We belong to the Lord and our very reason for living is not to please ourselves but to serve our Lord and minister to others."

Your home can be a Christian home and you can keep it that way if you will decide that that's the way it has to be.

Stand against the suggestion that you cannot be as true to the Lord as you used to be. This comes to every home. It comes to every teen-ager. High school and college years are those when you feel most keenly the pressure of the crowd around you. They say, "Don't be a square . . . don't be so old-fashioned. You can't do those things any more."

Your answer is "Who said so?" Human nature is still the same. The human heart is still the same. God is still the same. The Word of God is still the same and I can still be a Christian and I will!

You see, you don't have to give in to the suggestion that just because you live in the middle of the 20th century, you don't pray anymore, or that you don't sacrifice anymore, or that you don't live pure and clean anymore. Stand against this kind of compromise. Stand against the suggestion that it is old-fashioned and a square, odd-ball thing to read the Bible and pray together. Stand against the suggestion that it is old-fashioned to think a person ought to dress like a Christian and be modest and honor God in the way he dresses his body and the way he conducts himself in society. Stand against the suggestion that you have to let down simply because this is the 20th century.

You don't have to let down, you *can* live for God! And if you do, you'll be able to serve others in ways that those who compromise never could.

27. Specialize in Service

Specialize in service.

First of all, *in the home.* Paul says in Galatians 5:13 "You have been called to liberty, only use not your liberty as an occasion to the flesh, but by love serve one another."

By love serve one another.

And our Lord Jesus said in Mark 10:45—"For even the Son of man came not to be ministered unto but to minister, and to give his life a ransom for many."

Not to be ministered to but to minister.

These two verses, in combination, tell us what we ought to do in our home. There isn't any one person in the home who deserves to be served more than anyone else. In our American culture, of course, we pick out one day for Mother. On Mother's Day, we usually give her some presents . . . usually something she doesn't need and then, of course, we give her the privilege of cooking a big meal for the family. Everyone comes home on Mother's Day, so she has a chance to slave harder on that day.

But it's nice. We single her out for a little extra sentimental attention.

Later on, of course, we have Father's Day. On Father's Day, we generally give father a tie or something and tell him we are glad he is around and please keep on being at least solvent . . . so the home can go on. I'm just kidding you, Dad. But you know that's how it is.

Incidentally, did you happen to see the cartoon in which a wife was saying to her husband, "Oh, I wish you would make more money so I could give you more presents!"

That's a good one for Father's Day, isn't it?

We pick out special days . . . we have Children's Day, too.

243

All these different days, but this isn't the point of these Scriptures, and you know it.

Every day ought to be Mother's Day and every day ought to be Father's Day and every day ought to be Children's Day, in the Christian home.

By love serve one another.

What a surprise it would be if you actually did something for somebody in your home without having a reason. A friend of mine says that his youngsters will very frequently climb up on his lap and say "Daddy, I love you, you're the most wonderful daddy in the world." And they give him a big hug and kiss. But then he knows what's coming. "Please give me a dollar."

You see, they're doing something nice in order to get something out of father. Well, try surprising people. Try doing something nice that doesn't have any ulterior motive behind it. Just because you love the other person.

Serve one another, Paul says, by love.

The little loving touches mean so much!

Dr. Narramore was with us during a Bible conference and he told us that on one occasion when he had to go away on a trip, he was feeling sad and lonely because he had to leave his wife and little Melodie and the little boy, as all of us Dads do when we have to go away from home. When he reached his destination, he opened his suitcase and there, underneath one of his shirts was a little note which said "We miss you very much, but we love you." That was from his wife, Ruth.

Then, over among the socks there was a little note penned in the scrawl of a small child which was from Melodie. She said "Dear Daddy, we love you and we miss you. Hurry home."

Well, you know, that just made him know that he was loved and appreciated and it meant a lot to him.

Today, see what you can think of that you can do in your home, not because you have an ulterior motive, not because you want to get something out of somebody, but just because you love them and want to do something for them. It will help your home life tremendously.

Look for opportunities to be of help.

"How may I help?" ought to be the question, rather than "How may I get out of doing something?" This is particularly applicable to younger people who like to get out of work rather than to get into it. Don't wait to be asked to clear the table . . . get at it and help. Don't wait to be asked to carry out the trash . . . just volunteer.

There are a lot of things you can do without being asked that will make you a blessing in the home. Don't wait to be asked. It will help you in this matter of serving one another if you face realistically the problems that come up, instead of running away from them. Work out a plan that will be helpful to all concerned.

The answer to the question "How may I help?" oftentimes turns out to be "Stick with the problem and see it through instead of running away from it."

The mark of an immature person, whether husband or wife or son or daughter, is that he runs away from responsibility rather than facing it.

So, if you really love your family, you're going to face up to problems, not have a big knock-down, drag-out fight about it but face up to it realistically. You know . . . "this is how it is, what can we do about it?"

They say that worry is the absence of an organized plan. When you know what to do next, you don't worry so much about it.

The same thing is true of the tensions and the problems that we often face in our home. If we refuse to think about them realistically and face them, we're going to be worried and fretful and upset. But together, in love and by prayer, we can face up to our problems realistically. If we do that, we're going to find that things go better and that we are a help in our home.

Specialize in service in your home. How may I help? How may I be a blessing. Someone was complaining—I

think this was a Christian wife who wrote an article sometime ago—complaining that her husband, who is a minister
and a very good one, very seldom had any time to pray with
individuals in the home. He was praying with other people's
children, he was praying with other husbands' wives over
their problems, but he just never had time to pray about
anything in his own home.

This is a common problem, actually. It's not limited to the
occasional busy minister, God bless him, who has ulcers on
his ulcers and is trying to keep up with everying—but it is
true of many of us in the average Christian home. We get
busy about things . . . about our concerns and our worries
. . . about the responsibilities that we have outside. We forget
that those who are nearest and dearest to us oftentimes
would welcome a loving word, an earnest prayer, a little
encouragement from the Word of God and from a heart that
cares.

One other word before we leave this section. From time
to time you will do well to take inventory of your life as it
affects the other members of your family. What difference
are you making in their lives? Are you closer together in
spiritual things, or are you drifting apart? Have you been
taking enough time with each individual, or has someone
been neglected while you were—quite legitimately—busy
with other matters? Check up on yourself, and make sure
that *you* are serving and helping others as you should.

A wise person will study the other members of the home
circle, to discover their needs, and their desires and long-
ings. Then he will bend every effort to be of help and
encouragement in those key areas.

Specialize in service, not only *in* your home but *from* your
home.

The second point is . . . *from* your home.

Simon Peter said to his friends, as recorded in 1 Peter 4:9
"Use hospitality one to another without grudging."

And the writer to the Hebrews said, "Be not forgetful to
entertain strangers for some have entertained angels un-
aware."

And again in Hebrews 6:10, "God is not un-righteous to forget your work and labor of love which ye have showed toward his name, in that ye have ministered to the saints and do minister."

These are some of the verses that tell us of the value of using your home as a base for Christian service.

Paul mentions the household of Stephanus and said "They have addicted themselves to the ministry of the saints."

Then in this matter of soul winning, Paul says, "We preach not ourselves, but Christ Jesus as Lord and ourselves your servants for Jesus Christ."

Now here are some of the things you can do *from* your home.

First of all, *use your home as a base for encouraging believers,* especially those who have been recently converted. Bring the younger Christians (not only young in age, I mean, but someone who has recently found Christ)—bring a young Christian into your home and encourage him by prayer and hospitality and by showing him that someone cares.

Take another person who may have known the Lord for years but who is discouraged or having trouble . . . bring him into your home and bless him and help him and encourage him. You can use your home as a base for encouraging believers.

Somebody needs to be shown that you *care* what hap-pens in their lives.

Then *use your home as a base for reaching the unsaved.* "Use hospitality," Peter says.

Hospitality can be a means of winning souls.

Provide supper for that family that is just moving in or for the family across the way where the mother is sick and not able to prepare the evening meal. Bring your unsaved friends over, not just to preach to them but to have them in your home and let them feel the warmth and blessing of a Christian home. What your home is, often speaks louder than any sermon that you could preach. It speaks of Christ and that he is living in your life.

So use your home as a base for Christian service.

Many people nowadays are using their home as a base for a Bible class. They invite their neighbors in for a coffee klatch, for instance, or for an evening and they will open the Word of God and use their home as a base for Christian service.

Think it over. See what you can do in terms of using your home as a base from which to bless believers and from which you can preach the gospel to those who need to hear once again that Jesus Christ is the answer to their needs.

28. In Closing

It was in 1962 that I began my ministry as president of The King's College at Briarcliff Manor, New York. This independent, interdenominational and theologically conservative college had been founded by evangelist Percy Crawford in 1938. He continued to serve as president until his death in 1960.

"Walking with the King" during the years of responsibility as chief executive officer of a small Christian college has taught me some exceedingly valuable lessons.

God fits you for the task he gives you. Everything I had learned in the pastorate, in Youth for Christ, at Scripture Press, and in the "school of hard knocks" now came into sharp focus. I had needed all the insights I had gained along the way. Had I learned anything from preaching and pastoring? I was now shepherding a family of students, faculty, and staff of nearly a thousand souls.

Had I learned youth work and Christian promotion? I was now faced each day with the opportunity to interact with hundreds of eager young people, and to make the work of Christian higher education visible to the Christian community at large.

Had I learned how to manage and how to budget? I was now expected to keep a non-profit enterprise in the black, wipe out accumulated deficits, and seek and gain accreditation.

Had I learned to open the Word of God to people and give them a "handle" by which they could apply it to their lives? I was now given the chance to speak daily to many thousands by way of radio and gain cherished friends among a radio congregation—most of whom I would never meet this side of heaven. By now, my sign-off words, "Walk with the King today, and be a blessing!" are familiar to many homes.

What you are rubs off on the people with whom you live and work. Like many other parents, of course, I saw this happening in the lives of the children and precious grandchildren. Carolyn, now Mrs. Wendell Borrink, is the mother of Heidi Joy and Christopher Robert. Marilyn, now Mrs. John Parry, presented us with Melissa Coreen. In each of these lives I sometimes saw traces of my own shortcomings, and hopefully some evidence of blessing gained by God's grace along the way.

All along, I had observed that churches become a reflection of their pastors, and that institutions are often the lengthened shadow of their leadership. It is an awesome and frightening experience, however, to realize that your own people are picking up your personal traits. What I laughingly designated as "Cookisms" now cropped up in the conversation of others, and the principles which I applied in making management decisions came back to me promptly in the procedures of friends and co-workers. Again and again I have to learn that you cannot escape what you are, because it shows up in the lives of others.

God's timing is always right. In the beginning days at King's I was eager to see the college grow, and growth was indeed possible as the members of the post-World War II baby boom came of college age. Accordingly I encouraged the trustees to secure an architect, construct a master plan, and get under way. Soon the halls of the college were lined with blow-ups of architect's drawings.

The precarious financial history of the college and its exceedingly tight budget, however, prompted financial backers to say "Thanks, but no thanks." Our magnificent plan was stalled.

Undaunted, we grew as fast as we could, meanwhile putting our academic and financial house in order. We purchased additional property as it became available, and found the room to expand cautiously. The result was that while many colleges, using federal funds to build facilities for the apparently endless parade of student applicants, overspent and overbuilt. The result of these tendencies in some instances was financial disaster. Because King's chose a slower route we were able to stay fiscally and financially sound.

In God's time, not ours, came new buildings and facilities, with the money to fund them.

God gives what you ask. Two years before my 50th birthday, as a result of a conversation with Dr. Theodore Epp of "Back to the Bible," I began to seek the Lord for a new touch upon my life. As I prayed I besought my God for a new dimension, a new anointing, a new lease on life, so to speak, by my 50th birthday.

Then, suddenly, I was 50! In the pressure of transition from one job to another I had forgotten all about my half-century goal. Now, looking around me, I saw how wonderfully God had answered. One job finished, another begun. An exact duplication of the "next step" I had jotted on a 3 x 5 index card years before. I was indeed in "the school of God's choosing, where I might reproduce my ministry in the lives of young people." Furthermore, as I faced a position for which I had not been formally trained, I had been praying daily for God-given wisdom. Now I realized that a whole new set of insights had been given me, principles by which I could manage a challenging but oftentimes difficult situation. With it all, there was a joy and power that simply would not quit. God had given me that new touch, and I didn't even realize that it was happening!

The balance of power in any situation rests with people who pray. College life is not immune to the problems and short-comings of human nature; nor indeed to the occasional surfacing of pressure groups intent on accomplishing a special goal. It is a mistake to try confronting these problems in one's own strength or wisdom. Years ago I learned that one can, with blundering fingers, do immense damage to another under the guise of trying to "straighten him out." Rather, pray through a problem before you ever discuss it with another. By that time, your own soul will be cleansed and tender, and you will be used by the Spirit of God to accomplish what he wants.

The secret of a secure future is to keep producing all you can today. Physical endurance, nervous energy and capacity for sheer hard work under pressure may change as the years go by. In my 30s and 40s I could pray all night in an extended prayer meeting, be in meetings all the next day, and preach with power and blessing the following evening without any apparent strain. Just to think about it today is an effort. It is a mistake to try to reduplicate the energy or the looks and attitudes of youth. Be just what you are, but *be all you can be* each day as he fills and enables you. And be sure that you are producing creatively and up to your full capacity. You begin to die when you stop thinking and living productively. You can keep on living a full and satisfying life if you will insist each day on doing all you can, that day, by his grace. "It is God that worketh in you," said Paul. Let him work, then, each day, as you use your potential to the full for his glory.

One is only secure as long as someone needs him. So when we speak of producing, we are thinking of meeting the need of some other human being—and of doing so gladly, to the glory of God. T.J. Bach, of the Evangelical Alliance Mission used to say, "Walk softly, speak tenderly, don't run up stairs, and don't run down people!"

You don't ever succeed all by yourself—you need others. Just as surely as you find satisfaction and fulfillment only in meeting the needs of others, so you will discover that one succeeds only by the help of others. An advertising manual which I studied years ago began with the statement, "We exist by the consent of other people."

Nowhere has this truth been more evident than at The King's College. If it is true that no one can be good at everything, it also became evident that President Cook was going to have to secure knowledgeable help from a number of sources if he hoped to survive on the job.

I began to pray. I prayed for specific people with specific skills. And God began to send them my way. People came to work at King's at a personal cost of thousands of dollars a year. One professor, when asked why he chose King's over a salary paying twice as much, said, "Well, I guess you have to decide what you are willing to give up for Jesus, and then go and do it."

Today, after the years have gone by, and while one is still in the midstream of his ministry, "Walking with the King" turns out to be walking daily with his children . . . precious, loyal, loving, sacrificial people who are investing their lives in doing God's will.

Three things I pray: I hope never to live to see the day when I have lost the blessing of God. Nothing can match the sadness of the statement, "He wist not that the Lord was departed from him." The blessing of God means everything. I must have it each moment of each day, or die.

I pray always to love, to understand, and to help people. There is so much heartache, so many burdens in the lives of those around me. I pray always to be a help, not a hindrance.

I pray that I may always have something new and fresh from God's Word. Stale manna was useless and unpleasant, and so is stale preaching. As long as I live, I want to spill over some blessing from God's Word as I share the cup of life with others.

I guess what I have been saying is that I want to "Walk with the King today, and be a blessing!"